The Life Skills IQ Test

The Life Skills IQ Test

Test

10 Self-Quizzes to Measure Your Practical Intelligence

JOHN LIPTAK, EdD

BERKLEY BOOKS, NEW YORK

THE BERKLEY PUBLISHING GROUP
Published by the Penguin Group
Penguin Group (USA) Inc.
375 Hudson Street, New York, New York 10014, USA
Penguin Group (Canada), 90 Eglinton Avenue East, Suite 700, Toronto, Ontario M4P
2Y3, Canada (a division of Pearson Penguin Canada Inc.)
Penguin Books Ltd., 80 Strand, London WC2R 0RL, England
Penguin Group Ireland, 25 St. Stephen's Green, Dublin 2, Ireland
(a division of Penguin Books Ltd.)
Penguin Group (Australia), 250 Camberwell Road, Camberwell, Victoria 3124,
Australia (a division of Pearson Australia Group Pty. Ltd.)
Penguin Books India Pvt. Ltd., 11 Community Centre, Panchsheel Park, New Delhi—
110 017, India
Penguin Group (NZ), 67 Apollo Drive, Rosedale, North Shore 0632, New Zealand
(a division of Pearson New Zealand Ltd.)
Penguin Books (South Africa) (Pty.) Ltd., 24 Sturdee Avenue, Rosebank,
Johannesburg 2196, South Africa

Penguin Books Ltd., Registered Offices: 80 Strand, London WC2R 0RL, England

This publication is designed to provide accurate and authoritative information in
regard to the subject matter covered. It is sold with the understanding that the publisher
is not engaged in rendering legal, accounting, or other professional services. If you
require legal advice or other expert assistance, you should seek the services of a com-
petent professional. The publisher does not have any control over and does not assume
any responsibility for author or third-party websites or their content.

PRINTING HISTORY
Berkley trade paperback edition / October 2007

Library of Congress Cataloging-in-Publication Data

Liptak, John J.
    The life skills IQ test : 10 self-quizzes to measure your practical intelligence / by
John Liptak.
        p.   cm.
    ISBN 978-0-425-21714-6
    1. Intellect—Problems, exercises, etc.   2. Life skills—Problems, exercises, etc.
3. Self-evaluation.   I. Title.   II. Title: Life skills I.Q. test.
    BF431.3.L57 2007
    153.9—dc22

                                                                      2007005005

PRINTED IN THE UNITED STATES OF AMERICA

10 9 8 7 6 5 4 3 2 1

ACKNOWLEDGMENTS

There are so many people who have contributed to this book. I am deeply indebted to the hundreds of clients I have been privileged to work with over the years in the development of the Life Skills IQ approach. I would like to thank these people who, through sharing their stories and experiences, have taught me so much about the skills necessary to succeed in life and career.

I want to thank the following people for their generous contributions during the writing of this book. Most important, I am indebted to Jill Marsal of the Sandra Dijkstra Literary Agency, who understood the promise of this book from the beginning. She has contributed immeasurably to the overall quality of this book. I appreciate her friendship, her many great ideas, thought-provoking questions, and organizational assistance. Without her assistance, encouragement, and support, this book would not have been possible. I also appreciate the efforts of Taryn Fagerness for helping to make this book available in many foreign markets.

I would like to thank Denise Silvestro, executive editor at Berkley Publishing for believing in this book, and Katie Day, assistant editor at Berkley, for helping me polish the rough manuscript into a finished product. For their encouragement, care, attention to details, insight, and vision I am most grateful.

Finally, I would like to thank my wife, Kathy, who has supported me through this unique experience. I owe her a special debt of gratitude for her support, patience, and encouragement during the writing of this book.

CONTENTS

Introduction

Jim has trouble making important choices. He tends to make deci-
sions quickly and based on gut feelings. He rarely does any research
about the decision to be made, nor does he have a system for devel-
oping valid alternatives. Afterward, he often wonders if he could
have made a better decision or wishes he had taken more time to
deliberate.

Jill can't seem to hang on to a job for more than two years. She
often has trouble communicating, which leads to conflict in the
workplace. She inevitably gets in to arguments with her co-workers
and then quits soon after. Her way of dealing with conflict is to give
in to the other person, but that makes her feel bad about herself, so
she moves to another workplace in the hopes that things will be
better there.

Jane seems to never have enough money at the end of the
month. She tends to live from paycheck to paycheck, spending her
money as soon as it's deposited in her account. When she goes to the
mall, she tells herself that she will just look around and window-
shop, but when she gets there and sees things that she likes, she

can't resist. If she doesn't have cash to pay for the things, she uses her credit cards. Then she gets mad at herself because she has accumulated serious credit card debt.

Jim, Jill, and Jane have a variety of life problems. But they all share one important trait: They lack the essential life skills they need to change the emotional, behavioral, and cognitive patterns that cause them anxiety, stress, and general unhappiness. Life skills are those invaluable, everyday skills that, if used effectively, allow you to access the inner resources you need to succeed and create the life you desire. Life skills are the necessary skills that help you take charge of your personal and professional life, manage change, and deal effectively with your environment and the people in that environment. At their most basic, life skills are the daily living skills you need to be happy, healthy, and successful.

We all have a certain amount of life skills—we'd be totally dysfunctional people without them. But skills differ from person to person, as do our abilities to put them to use. Your Life Skills IQ is your individual degree of effectiveness in using your life skills, a measure of how well you're actually able to apply them to your daily life. This book will help you determine your Life Skills IQ by evaluating your competency in ten critical life skills areas: interpersonal interaction style, communication skills, assertiveness, decision-making effectiveness, leisure participation, money management, time management, positive relationships, conflict resolution, and emotional management. It will provide you with a personalized life skills profile that will help you identify the skills you lack, and refine those you already have. Even more important, it will show you how to use your Life Skills IQ to improve every aspect of your life.

But before we begin, I want to give you some more background on the concept of life skills, and of intelligence testing in general.

INTELLIGENCE TESTING

Almost every one of us has taken a traditional Intelligence Quotient (IQ) test at some point in our lives. We've made our way through a collection of bizarre verbal and visual puzzles, only to come up with a score, some indicator of our raw intelligence level, a prediction of how well we will fare in our professional lives.

Although intelligence tests have been refined and improved over time, the notion that one score could have a significant effect on a person's life has always been controversial. Many recent scholars have suggested that the notion of the IQ is antiquated and needs to be replaced by a more modern way of thinking. Howard Gardener, a developmental psychologist at Harvard, has suggested the notion of multiple intelligences to reflect the notion that intelligence is made up of many facets. Similarly, Robert Sternberg has developed a theory of intelligence that includes what he calls "practical intelligence," or common sense intelligence.

The premise of this book is that, as modern psychology suggests, intelligence about daily life skills may actually be more important than having a high IQ. In other words, instead of focusing on a "traditional" level of intelligence as a benchmark for success, you need to develop the life skills necessary to change the emotional, behavioral, and thinking patterns that cause you problems in your daily life. Remember: Unlike the knowledge measured by traditional IQ tests, life skills can be learned or refined, growing as you build into a more successful, satisfying, and productive life. It's your Life Skills Intelligence that will help you tangibly improve your life—and that's just what this book is designed to show you.

LIFE SKILLS INTELLIGENCE

In keeping with what modern psychology suggests, I believe there are several kinds of intelligence that contribute to your overall life skills intelligence:

SPIRITUAL INTELLIGENCE is concerned with issues of meaning, values, and purpose; interest in the importance of and search for clarity; the search for greater meaning in life; a commitment to faith and optimism; interest in developing the inner self and identifying purpose to life; and an ability to see the whole picture, not just isolated events.

PHYSICAL INTELLIGENCE looks at nutritional practices, interest in regular exercise, consistent and adequate sleep, practical and effective use of relaxation and meditation techniques, optimism about one's ability to take care of health problems, and respect for one's own body.

MENTAL INTELLIGENCE examines the ability to engage in clear thinking and the recollection of information with minimal interference from emotional baggage, the ability to think independently and critically, possession of basic reasoning skills, being open to new ideas, knowledge of one's cultural heritage, and an interest in lifelong learning.

EMOTIONAL INTELLIGENCE deals with awareness of one's emotions; the ability to maintain control over emotional states, including appropriate emotional responses in reaction to life events; the ability to experience happiness and positive emotional states; and the ability to understand one's feelings.

SOCIAL INTELLIGENCE is concerned with sharing intimacy, friendship, and membership in groups; the ability to practice active listening and empathy; the interest shown in caring for others; and being open to caring and showing commitment to the common good of people, community, and the world.

CAREER INTELLIGENCE focuses on maximizing one's skills and abilities; the ability to maintain a sense of control over the occupational demands in the workplace; a balance between time and energy spent at work, with family, and at leisure; knowledge of one's interests, values, and personality; and knowledge of workplace politics, policies, and procedures.

Over the course of this book, we're going to touch on all of those types of intelligences by means of various life skills *assessments* (or inventories), which I'll talk more about shortly.

I also believe it's of the utmost importance that we recognize the way we fall into specific behavioral patterns, based on how effectively we use our life skills. Remember Jim, Jill, and Jane from the beginning of the introduction? They all had one thing in common—they repeated their behaviors over and over again, regardless of the results they kept getting. The fact is, we all live our lives according to certain life skills patterns that have been conditioned from an early age, perhaps even from birth. Patterns that are completely unconscious. Some are positive and productive, but others—as in the cases of our three friends—are serious barriers to life and career success.

That's where your Life Skills IQ comes in. When you're having success in life, you naturally keep doing what works. You probably manage your time and money well, communicate effectively with others, resolve conflicts and make good decisions, and successfully manage your emotions. Your patterns allow you to be effective and efficient in living your life, thus you have a high Life Skills IQ. On the other hand, when you keep repeating patterns that are ineffective uses of your life skills, your situation begins to break down. These negative life skills patterns manifest themselves in trouble maintaining relationships with other people, having career problems, not effectively managing your time, giving up easily, working to avoid other things or people in your life—generally, when your life just doesn't seem to have the flow it should. All of those unfortunate things indicate that you have a low Life Skills IQ.

Whether or not they're effective in helping you achieve your goals, life skills have a tendency to keep repeating themselves if they are left unexamined. That's the reason so many people go through life repeatedly using ineffective life skills, expecting different results each time. But I'm here to tell you that, once you have identified these negative patterns, you will have the power to alter them so that you begin to experience positive rather than negative results.

LIFE SKILLS BUILDING

This book is based on the notion that, by engaging in self-reflection, you can develop and strengthen your Life Skills IQ. I call this process Life Skills Building (LSB), an educational process intended to empower you to develop better skills for living. LSB is founded on the belief that people who develop better skills for living will take more responsibility for their own lives and careers. The purpose of LSB is to help people develop greater skill strengths, which can be used to address current concerns and prevent similar patterns from occurring in the future.

As human beings, we possess the desire to know ourselves and find meaning in our lives. We are the only creatures on earth who can reflect on ourselves and our lives and attempt to make meaningful changes to them. Life Skills Building provides you with a structured method to undertake that self-examination, to really look at the patterns in your own life. LSB allows you to further understand who you are; explore your personal characteristics and tendencies, lifestyle choices, and attitudes; and identify, analyze, and alter the negative patterns that keep reoccurring in your life. In that way, Life Skills Building helps free you from the grip that negative patterns have on you.

The LSB in this book is based on four principles:

1. You need to set aside time to self-reflect. *You need time to read this book, complete the assessments contained in it, and answer the journal questions.*
2. You need some sort of structure that encourages

you to examine the patterns in your life. *The assessments in this book will provide you with the necessary structure to reflect on the negative patterns affecting the flow of your life.*

3. You need to journal about your past to better understand how the negative patterns have formed. *The journaling exercises contained in this book will allow you to examine the forces that have contributed to behavior that keeps you from being happy and successful.*

4. Lastly, you need to make behavioral changes, based on the information and knowledge you have gathered about yourself.

Life Skills Building is not an easy task; it requires you to pay attention to things you've never thought about before. It requires you to explore your weaknesses as well as your strengths. But in the end, whatever discomfort you feel while working on your LSB will prove to be worthwhile. You will be shocked at how much you can improve the quality of your life by learning more about yourself.

LIFE SKILLS ASSESSMENTS

The tools you will use to tackle your LSB are the assessments provided in this book. After reading and completing the assessments and activities, you will have a holistic and honest understanding of your spiritual, physical, mental, emotional, social, career, and overall Life Skills Intelligences. These assessments constitute the equipment you will use on your journey of self-exploration, tools that will allow you to seek, ponder, evaluate, invent, and reinvent yourself, and start viewing yourself in a realistic manner. They are the means by which you will learn to:

- accept all aspects of your personality
- celebrate your strengths and identify your weaknesses
- make effective decisions based on knowledge about yourself
- make a commitment to enhance or alter ineffective patterns in your life
- take action to make the necessary changes in your life
- gain insight and a "wake-up call" for behavioral change
- explore the effects of unconscious childhood messages
- uncover resources you possess that can help you to better cope with problems

In other words, really put your life skills to work.

TAKING THE ASSESSMENTS

The assessments or inventories in this book have been developed and designed just like any other test, inventory, or assessment on the market (and are similar to the ones used by psychologists, counselors, and career consultants, which would cost you hundreds of dollars to take and have interpreted). They are designed to be self-administered, self-scored, and self-interpreted, meaning the assessment interpretations are based on self-reported data. In other words, the accuracy and usefulness of the information I provide is dependent on the honest and truthful information you provide about yourself. You may not learn much from taking some of the inventories—you may simply verify some information that you already know. On the other hand, you may uncover information that's keeping you from being as happy or successful as you should be. Either way, the important thing is that you are honest about yourself.

Please remember: An assessment instrument can provide you with valuable information about yourself, but it cannot measure or identify everything about you. Its purpose is not to pigeonhole you with certain characteristics, but rather to allow you to explore all your traits. Remember, too, that this book contains assessments, not "traditional" tests. Tests measure knowledge or whether something is right or wrong. For the assessments in this book, there are no right or wrong answers. You'll only be asked for your opinions and attitudes about important life topics.

In each of the following ten chapters, you'll be asked to complete one comprehensive opening assessment or inventory. Write directly in the book.

Please try to complete the assessment as honestly as possible. Remember, these tests will make you more aware of your strengths and weaknesses, personal characteristics, and beliefs; allow you to see the structure of very distinct life patterns; and provide you with deep insight into yourself and others.

When you're finished, score the assessment and use your results to determine your life skills profile. (You will have directions for scoring your specific life skills assessments and interpretation materials to help you determine what your scores mean.)

There are a few other important things to remember:

- Take your time completing the inventories. There is no time limit, so work at your own pace.
- Find a quiet place where you can complete the assessments without being disturbed.
- Before completing each inventory, be sure to read the specific instructions. Each assessment has a different format with different scoring instructions and methods for self-interpretation.
- Keep an eye out for additional self-directed journaling activities, which will assist you in the self-discovery process.
- Always keep in mind that the assessments contained in this book are designed to be exploratory in nature. They are merely a starting point for you to begin learning more about yourself and how you fit into the world. You may not always agree with the outcomes of all inventories, but do not get upset. Remember that this is merely an exploratory exercise, not a final definition of your characteristics or attitudes.
- Have fun! The purpose of the assessments is for you to learn about yourself in a nonthreatening way.
- Lastly, and most important, remember that these inventories are not a substitute for professional assistance. If you feel you need professional assistance, please consult a mental health professional or a professional career counselor.

By the end of the book, you'll have a comprehensive view of yourself based on ten critical life skills—an assessment of your Life Skills IQ. Armed with that information, you'll learn how to turn knowledge into action; how to change your patterns and behaviors; and improve your personal, professional, and social lives.

Let's get started!

one

Interpersonal Interactions

RELATE WELL BY DEVELOPING INTERPERSONAL EXPERTISE

There is no one best way for interacting with other people, but overall, the goal of interpersonal interaction is to establish effective communication with another person. Effective communication occurs when you and the other person are totally in sync, fully connected, and comfortable in sharing feelings, thoughts, and ideas. When this happens, you can be more creative and enthusiastic about what you're trying to communicate. Effective interaction helps you to connect with other people and gives your relationships meaning and depth.

Problems with communication and interpersonal interaction occur when people use different *styles* of interacting. You may like to use lots of concrete facts when you're speaking, but the person you're speaking to might be a more abstract and conceptual thinker, relying more on feelings and emotions than hard facts. Because his interaction style is different, he might have trouble understanding you. Therefore, it is very important for you to determine your dominant interpersonal style and learn to recognize the interpersonal styles of others, so that you can work to establish the most effective communication possible.

The Interpersonal Interactions Inventory (III) can help you identify the characteristics that define your interactions with others. By understanding more about your interaction style, you will learn how you can more effectively deal with other people, achieve greater job satisfaction, and make better life decisions.

INTERPERSONAL INTERACTIONS INVENTORY

The Interpersonal Interactions Inventory (III) will help you explore how you interact with other people. This assessment contains forty-four statements. Read each of the statements and decide how much you agree. In each of the choices listed, circle the number of your response on the line to the right of each statement.

In the following example, the circled *1* indicates that the statement is not true of the person completing the scale:

	VERY TRUE	SOMEWHAT TRUE	NOT TRUE
1. I enjoy orderly, organized environments.	3	2	①

Typically, people fall into one of four categories of interaction and communication styles (though there can be some overlap): Concrete Communicators, Spontaneous Communicators, Intellectual Communicators, and Sensitive Communicators. These styles make up the four scales on the III, the scales being the system I use to group answers to help you to explore your specific communication style more easily. After you determine your scores and identify the specific scale on which you scored highest, there will be an in-depth profile of each style.

Remember, this is not a test. Since there are no right or wrong answers, do not spend too much time thinking about your responses. Be sure to respond to every statement.

	VERY TRUE	SOMEWHAT TRUE	NOT TRUE
1. I enjoy orderly, organized environments.	3	2	1
2. I am adventurous and fun-loving.	3	2	1
3. I value intelligence in myself and in others.	3	2	1
4. I am warm-hearted and empathetic.	3	2	1
5. I need clearly defined rules and guidelines.	3	2	1
6. I have trouble saving money for the future.	3	2	1
7. I am analytical and insightful.	3	2	1
8. I want to work where I can be creative.	3	2	1
9. I am responsible and hard-working.	3	2	1
10. I love surprises and the unexpected.	3	2	1
11. I tend to be impersonal and aloof.	3	2	1
12. I invest a lot of emotion and time in my relationships.	3	2	1
13. I take personal commitments very seriously.	3	2	1
14. I like immediate gratification.	3	2	1
15. I utilize logic and objectivity.	3	2	1
16. I enjoy harmony and dislike conflict.	3	2	1
17. I have a tendency to be controlling and inflexible.	3	2	1
18. I do not like routine or structure.	3	2	1

19. I like to debate with other people.	3	2	1
20. I like to understand and express my deepest feelings.	3	2	1
21. I mostly communicate about concrete, observable information.	3	2	1
22. I am adaptable and flexible.	3	2	1
23. I am skeptical about most things.	3	2	1
24. I tend to take things very personally.	3	2	1
25. I am loyal and dependable.	3	2	1
26. I live in the present and do not worry about the past or future.	3	2	1
27. I do not place much value on relationships.	3	2	1
28. I will usually take the side of the "underdog."	3	2	1
29. I am rarely impulsive or spontaneous.	3	2	1
30. I am spontaneous and trust my intuition.	3	2	1
31. I have strong convictions and principles.	3	2	1
32. I get bored with things after the initial excitement wears off.	3	2	1
33. I worry about unpredictable events.	3	2	1
34. I am practical and pragmatic.	3	2	1
35. I understand and see patterns in complex information.	3	2	1
36. I am idealistic about life.	3	2	1
37. I am accurate and detail-oriented.	3	2	1
38. I value freedom and autonomy.	3	2	1
39. I want to make unique contributions in my work.	3	2	1
40. I have a vision of the ideal world and work toward that.	3	2	1
41. I make financial sacrifices for future security.	3	2	1

42. I like work to be exciting and fun.   3   2   1

43. I connect more with others' minds than

     their hearts.   3   2   1

44. I readily share my personal values and

     dreams.   3   2   1

SCORING DIRECTIONS

The Interpersonal Interactions Inventory is designed to measure the style you most often use when communicating and interacting with others, which has a lot to do with how successful you are in life, in your career, and with family and friends. Scoring the III is a very easy process. Look at the questions you just answered. Use the spaces below to record the number that you circled for each question. Then, calculate the sum for each of the columns (scales) and put that total underneath each column.

SCALE 1	SCALE 2	SCALE 3	SCALE 4
1 _____	2 _____	3 _____	4 _____
5 _____	6 _____	7 _____	8 _____
9 _____	10 _____	11 _____	12 _____
13 _____	14 _____	15 _____	16 _____
17 _____	18 _____	19 _____	20 _____
21 _____	22 _____	23 _____	24 _____
25 _____	26 _____	27 _____	28 _____
29 _____	30 _____	31 _____	32 _____
33 _____	34 _____	35 _____	36 _____

37 _____	38 _____	39 _____	40 _____
41 _____	42 _____	43 _____	44 _____
TOTAL	TOTAL	TOTAL	TOTAL
_____	_____	_____	_____
CONCRETE COMMUNICATORS	SPONTANEOUS COMMUNICATORS	INTELLECTUAL COMMUNICATORS	SENSITIVE COMMUNICATORS

INTERPRETING YOUR SCORES

As we've established, people have different ways of communicating: Some like to deal with facts, others enjoy high-energy interactions, others like talking about abstract and conceptual ideas, and still others value talking about feelings. Problems in relationships often stem from two or more people trying to communicate using different interpersonal interaction styles.

The III helps you explore your preferred communication style—the one you typically use when communicating with others. Look at the profile interpretations below. The area in which you scored the highest tends to be your preferred interpersonal interaction style. However, you may find that you have scored high on two scales. If this is the case, it means that you probably are able to switch back and forth between the two styles based on the situation you find yourself in. In this case, you should read the interpretation provided for both interpersonal interaction styles. Similarly, the area in which you scored the lowest tends to be your least preferred interpersonal interaction style.

Read about all of the interpersonal interaction styles to help you better understand the ways in which we all interact.

Then, complete the exercises to help you learn more about your interaction style, and how you can integrate other styles into your own to better communicate with the people around you.

SCORES FROM 11 TO 18 ARE LOW and indicate that you do not use this interpersonal interaction style very often. You should think of different ways that you can develop and use communication techniques from this style.

SCORES FROM 19 TO 25 ARE AVERAGE and indicate that you use this interpersonal interaction style some of the time. You should think of ways to incorporate more of the communication techniques from this interpersonal interaction style.

SCORES FROM 26 TO 33 ARE HIGH and mean that you use this interpersonal interaction style most of the time. You should be aware that you are relying too much on the communication techniques from this style and think of ways to incorporate the best communication techniques from the other three interpersonal interaction styles.

SCALE DESCRIPTIONS

CONCRETE COMMUNICATORS

You enjoy thinking and talking about concrete, tangible, observable information. When you are communicating with other people, you like it when things are stated clearly and make sense to you. You enjoy specifics and do not like to talk about things that are abstract or force you to search for hidden meanings. You rarely enjoy talking about theoretical concepts or abstract ideas. You enjoy gathering and using information in a practical way. You prefer brief interactions that get straight to the point. You are not interested in information or conversation that is vague or impractical. You are detail-oriented, focused, and very analytical in your communication with others. You are very good at organizing your thoughts and planning what you say. You tend to be somewhat rigid in your thinking and can be narrow-minded.

Answer the following questions to learn more about yourself and your interpersonal interaction style:

You often assume that your way is the only way to do things. How does this affect your relationships with significant others?

_____

_____

_____

_____

You are often a rigid thinker and don't want or don't trust the ideas and opinions of other people. Describe times when you have ruled out other people's ideas or opinions because you thought they were too unrealistic:

_____

_____

_____

_____

You have trouble expressing appreciation for the efforts of others. Describe times when you could have been more appreciative and how you can begin to recognize and appreciate the efforts of others:

_____

_____

_____

_____

You love examining minute details. Describe a time when you were so worried about the details that you did not enjoy the activity you were participating in:

_____

_____

_____

_____

You do not like to express your feelings to other people. Describe a situation in which you wished you had been able to express intimate feelings to a significant other:

_____

_____

_____

_____

You like everything planned in advance. How could you start being more spontaneous in your interactions with others?

_____

_____

_____

_____

SPONTANEOUS COMMUNICATORS

You enjoy communicating in an action-oriented, hands-on environment that stimulates your senses. You tend to take what people say literally and at face value, and to communicate with an easy, informal style that people enjoy. Your language tends to be uncomplicated and down-to-earth. You have lots of energy and get frustrated when trapped in a long conversation. You are open-minded about the types of conversation topics you entertain. You are often unable to sit down for quiet conversation times. You love situations that are unpredictable and allow you to be spontaneous. You tend to be the life of the party in social situations. You love being around people and tend to be a magnet for others. You can become silly if you become too spontaneous.

Answer the following questions to learn more about yourself and your interpersonal interaction style:

You need variety, excitement, and adventure in your life and in your relationships. How have these needs stopped you from developing relationships or stopped you from further developing established relationships?

_____

_____

_____

_____

You tend to have a high level of energy. In your communications, you tend to use a lot of hand gestures and may ramble too much. How has this energy level both helped and hurt you?

_____

_____

_____

_____

Because you have so much energy and enthusiasm, you often "smother" friends and family. Describe times when being overly friendly has hurt your relationships with others:

_____

_____

_____

_____

You have very short-term interests, and your conversations tend to jump from topic to topic. What can you do to maintain sustained interest in certain people or topics?

_____

_____

_____

_____

You exhibit a carefree demeanor. What things or people do you care most about? How can you better show them how you feel?

_____

_____

_____

_____

You are unable to sit quietly for long periods of time. How can you learn to enjoy the deeper and quieter aspects of life?

_____

_____

_____

_____

INTELLECTUAL COMMUNICATORS

You enjoy thinking and talking about abstract, conceptual ideas and events. You tend to enjoy talking about possibilities rather than facts or reality. When you are communicating, you tend to focus on inconsistencies and logical flaws in your own and others' speech and thinking. Your language tends to be complex and scholarly. You are able to quickly and efficiently move from a single thought to a larger pattern that reflects your philosophy of life. You tend to communicate very intuitively, often jumping from one thought to another as you see fit. You are willing to risk having your thoughts and ideas rejected by others. You may appear aloof in some social situations because you enjoy intellectual conversations.

Answer the following questions to learn more about your-self and your interpersonal interaction style:

Sometimes you can be silent, cold, or resistant in social situations. How can you overcome this behavior?

_____

_____

_____

_____

You like to engage in intellectually stimulating conversations about theoretical concepts. What are some concrete topics that you might enjoy talking to others about?

_____

_____

_____

_____

You are always objective and levelheaded. What are some situations where these attributes might work against you?

_____

_____

_____

_____

You can become overwhelmed by verbally discussing your feelings. In the space, describe some of your innermost feelings:

_____

_____

_____

_____

You tend to be very serious. What are some nonintellectual activities in which you would like to engage?

_____

_____

_____

_____

You like to have a logical reason for all that you do and say. List several things you would like to do or say that are more spontaneous:

_____

_____

_____

_____

SENSITIVE COMMUNICATORS

You enjoy thinking and talking about feelings and matters of the heart. You tend to talk about possibilities and what might be in the future, rather than what is in the present. You enjoy discussing your private thoughts, fantasies, spirituality, and life philosophies with other people. You rarely care about concrete, factual information. You are very sensitive to subtle nuances in communication such as a person's body language, facial expressions, and vocal intonations. You tend to be very good at reading between the lines, understanding empathetically what other people are saying, and perceiving underlying meanings in others' words. Your communication is imaginative, filled with metaphors and analogies. Through sharing feelings, you are better able to connect with other people.

Answer the following questions to learn more about yourself and your interpersonal interaction style:

You tend to be overly sensitive to what others say and do and you seem to be overly concerned with not hurting others' feelings or being hurt by others. Describe what you think happens when others do not approve of you or something you do:

_____
_____
_____
_____

You are often afraid of disagreements. Describe situations in which you probably should have stood up for yourself, but did not:

_____
_____
_____
_____

You are not very assertive. Describe the people with whom you feel you need to be more assertive. Describe a situation with one of these people in which you would like to be more assertive in the future:

_____

_____

_____

_____

You often provide a sympathetic ear to others. What things can you do to get others to provide a sympathetic ear to you when the need arises?

_____

_____

_____

_____

You read other people very well. What do you think your body language says when you are communicating?

_____

_____

_____

_____

You are very open with your inner thoughts and feelings. Describe a situation where that has been or might be troublesome:

_____

_____

_____

_____

EXERCISES AND ACTIVITIES

What is your primary Interpersonal Interaction Style (styles if you had a high score on two different scales):

_____

_____

What Interpersonal Interaction Style did your mother/primary female caregiver use and how has that affected your interpersonal style?

_____

_____

_____

_____

What Interpersonal Interaction Style did your father/primary male caregiver use and how has that affected your interpersonal style?

_____

_____

_____

_____

What Interpersonal Interaction Style do you think is best and why?

_____

_____

_____

_____

What changes would you like to make to your Interpersonal Interactions Style?

_____

_____

_____

_____

What do you like best about the Interpersonal Interaction Style you are currently using?

_____

_____

_____

_____

How could you be a better communicator?

_____

_____

_____

_____

How can knowledge of your Interpersonal Interaction Style improve your relationships?

_____

_____

_____

_____

How is each style effective in certain situations?

_____

_____

_____

_____

DIFFERENT STYLES FOR DIFFERENT SITUATIONS

Think about the different situations in which it would be useful to use a certain interaction style. For example, when talking with a significant other about choosing a car, the concrete, fact-based communication style might be the most effective. However, when discussing your life together, the sensitive communication style might be the most effective. In the space below, list situations where the identified style would be most effective.

INTERPERSONAL INTERACTION STYLE	EFFECTIVE SITUATIONS
Concrete Communicators	
Spontaneous Communicators	
Intellectual Communicators	
Sensitive Communicators	

USING ALL STYLES

In order to interact effectively, you must learn to use all of the different interpersonal interaction styles—which means you must be able to identify the styles that you and the other person are exhibiting, match your style to the other person's, and communicate appropriately. Pick six people you know. Write down their primary interpersonal interaction style and your ideas for how you can better communicate with each of them.

PERSON I KNOW	INTERPERSONAL INTERACTION STYLE	WAYS TO COMMUNICATE BETTER

SOCIAL SITUATIONS

Social situations are the best opportunities for you to practice using communication techniques from different interpersonal interaction styles. Think about and write down an upcoming social situation: _____

List five interpersonal traits you do not have, but you will work on improving during this event:

INTERPERSONAL TRAITS	HOW I WILL IMPROVE

two

Communication Skills

All people have needs—whether personal, social, or business related—that can only be satisfied by communicating with other human beings. Communication is the foundation for all interpersonal interactions and relationships; our daily lives are filled with a variety of communication experiences. The question is: How useful and fulfilling are those communication experiences?

True, effective communication allows you to understand other people, influence others, learn from others, and learn more about yourself. Interpersonal communication describes those activities that involve interactions between two or more people—in essence, it is what allows you to begin and maintain relationships with other people. I measure communication effectiveness by the quality of your attitude toward others; the effectiveness of your speaking, language, and listening skills; and your ability to listen effectively and understand others.

I want to emphasize that communication skills are the most important life skills you can develop because they allow you to connect and stay connected with people in your home, your community, and the world. The Communication Skills Possession Inventory (CSPI) will help you identify your interpersonal strengths and weaknesses, and explore how good of a communicator you are when listening to or talking to other people.

COMMUNICATION SKILLS POSSESSION INVENTORY

For the forty items contained in this inventory, read each of the statements and decide how descriptive it is of you. In the following example, the circled *3* indicates that the statement was somewhat descriptive of the person completing the inventory.

4 = VERY DESCRIPTIVE	3 = SOMEWHAT DESCRIPTIVE	2 = A LITTLE DESCRIPTIVE	I = NOT AT ALL DESCRIPTIVE

When talking to others:

1. I speak with respect for the other person.   4   ③   2   1

Because communication is much more than simply talking to others, the CSPI can help you to identify those areas in which you communicate well and those areas where you might need to improve. For each of the sections you complete, count the sum total of the scores you circled for each of the four sections. Put that total on the line marked "Total" at the end of each section. Remember, this is not a test. Since there are no right or wrong answers, do not spend too much time thinking about your answers. Be sure to respond to every statement.

4 = VERY DESCRIPTIVE	3 = SOMEWHAT DESCRIPTIVE	2 = A LITTLE DESCRIPTIVE	I = NOT AT ALL DESCRIPTIVE

1. When talking to others:

1. I am willing to share personal information.	4	3	2	1
2. I am open to listening to others share personal information.	4	3	2	1
3. I am willing to risk rejection from others.	4	3	2	1
4. I am interested in what others feel and think.	4	3	2	1
5. I listen in an accepting way.	4	3	2	1
6. I accept other people regardless of what information they share.	4	3	2	1
7. I disclose my intimate feelings if appropriate.	4	3	2	1
8. I will disclose aspects of my past if the time is appropriate.	4	3	2	1
9. I support others when they share personal information about themselves.	4	3	2	1
10. I self-disclose positive and negative aspects of myself.	4	3	2	1

SELF-DISCLOSURE TOTAL = _____

2. When talking to others:

11. I make attempts to develop trust with them.	4	3	2	1
12. I use personal pronouns when communicating.	4	3	2	1
13. I talk about facts and do not engage in gossip.	4	3	2	1
14. I allow them to state their opinions and points of view.	4	3	2	1
15. I listen attentively to what they are saying.	4	3	2	1
16. I restate their point of view to show them I understand.	4	3	2	1

17. I make every attempt to understand their ideas
    and feelings.   4   3   2   1
18. I use nonverbal behavior to express my feelings
    and attitudes.   4   3   2   1
19. I organize my thoughts before speaking.   4   3   2   1
20. I assert myself to get what I want, but not at their expense. 4   3   2   1

BUILDING TRUST TOTAL = _____

3. When talking to others:

21. I say what I am feeling.   4   3   2   1
22. I am often aware in my body what I am feeling.   4   3   2   1
23. I express my feelings in an appropriate manner.   4   3   2   1
24. I listen to the message and the feelings behind the words. 4   3   2   1
25. I communicate my feelings through my body language.   4   3   2   1
26. I am able to control my anger.   4   3   2   1
27. I describe my angry feelings in an appropriate manner. 4   3   2   1
28. I am aware of the thoughts that trigger negative emotions. 4   3   2   1
29. I make sure that my verbal and nonverbal messages
    are the same.   4   3   2   1
30. I do not hold negative feelings inside, but I express
    them appropriately.   4   3   2   1

COMMUNICATING FEELINGS TOTAL = _____

4. When talking to others:

31. I value diversity as an important resource.   4   3   2   1
32. I respect their cultural and ethnic heritage.   4   3   2   1
33. I constantly work to reduce my cultural biases.   4   3   2   1
34. I avoid terms that devalue others.   4   3   2   1
35. I try not to react to others in a stereotypical way. 4   3   2   1

36. I use language that is appropriate to people
   from all cultures.   4 3 2 1
37. I anticipate how my messages will be interpreted by
   the listener.   4 3 2 1
38. I believe diversity can add to productivity and creativity. 4 3 2 1
39. I am aware of my own historical and cultural
   background.   4 3 2 1
40. I commit considerable time and energy to relations
   with people different from me.   4 3 2 1

VALUING DIVERSITY TOTAL = _____

SCORING DIRECTIONS

If you have not scored the inventory yet, total the scores you circled for each of the four sections. Put that total on the line marked "Total" at the end of each section.

Then, transfer your totals to the spaces below:

TOTALS

1. _____ Self-Disclosure (Disclosing personal aspects of yourself to others)
2. _____ Building Trust (The ability to trust other people, and have other people trust you)
3. _____ Communicating Feelings (The ability to share your feelings with other people)
4. _____ Valuing Diversity (The ability to understand and accept other people for who they are)

INTERPRETING YOUR SCORES

SCORES FROM 10 TO 19 ARE LOW and indicate that you need to improve your communication skills.

SCORES FROM 20 TO 30 ARE AVERAGE and indicate that you have communication skills similar to others taking this assessment.

SCORES FROM 31 TO 40 ARE HIGH and indicate that you have mastered this area of communication.

For any scales on which you scored in the "Low" range, find that description on the pages that follow. Then, read the description and complete the included exercises. These will help you develop more effective communication skills.

SCALE DESCRIPTIONS

SELF-DISCLOSURE

Self-disclosure is when you disclose your feelings and thoughts to other people. This creates the potential for trust, commitment, caring, understanding, and growth. But to be effective in disclosing yourself to others, you must first be emotionally open to them. When you are open, you will let others know who you are as a person.

Think about some of the people you know and those you

would like to know better. Answer the following questions
with them in mind:

Who would you like to get to know?

_____

_____

_____

_____

With whom would you like to deepen your relationship?

_____

_____

_____

_____

What interests, activities, and goals do you have in common
with other people in your life?

_____

_____

_____

_____

How can you disclose information about these interests, activities, and goals to the other people in your life?

_____

_____

_____

_____

What types of things would you like to "get off your chest" by
disclosing them to other people in your life?

_____

_____

_____

_____

In the following spaces, practice disclosing personal information:

Person with whom I would like to deepen my relationship:	
Things I could disclose to this person:	
Feelings I would like to share with this person:	
What I would learn or better understand about myself:	

EXERCISES AND ACTIVITIES

Self-disclosure Questionnaire

Having material to self-disclose is critical in developing inter-personal relationships. The following questions are designed to provide you with information for self-disclosure in conversations with other people:

1. What fond memories do you have of your childhood?

_____

_____

_____

_____

2. What makes you feel the most uncomfortable?

_____

_____

_____

_____

3. Whom do you trust most? Why?

_____

_____

_____

_____

4. What is your primary life goal?

_____

_____

_____

_____

5. What have you always dreamed of doing?

_____

_____

_____

_____

6. What has been your favorite job? Why?

_____

_____

_____

_____

7. What do you value the most?

_____

_____

_____

_____

8. What do you wish you did better?

_____

_____

_____

_____

BUILDING TRUST

To develop and maintain effective relationships with other people, you must establish trust. People who score high on this scale are able to build and foster caring and productive relationships. They communicate accurate and relevant information, and are quite willing to openly share their thoughts and feelings with others. Trustworthy people are likely to take risks and communicate with friendliness and spontaneity; they behave ethically and morally in their relationships. They also are able to build effective relationships with people from diverse cultures. They avoid stereotyping others and value differences in the people with whom they have relationships. Trustworthy people express acceptance, support, and cooperation with others.

What are some of the most important things you can do to develop trust?

_____

_____

_____

_____

What can you do to begin ensuring people trust you more?

_____

_____

_____

_____

PEOPLE I TRUST

In the following space, write the names of people in your life whom you trust and why. These people can be family, friends, neighbors, co-workers, etc.

PEOPLE I TRUST	WHY

PEOPLE WHO DO NOT TRUST ME

In the following space, write the names of people in your life who do not trust you and why. These people can be family, friends, neighbors, co-workers, etc.

PEOPLE WHO DO NOT TRUST ME	WHY THEY DO NOT TRUST ME

LISTENING

The ability to listen to others with whom you are communicating is critical in developing deep and long-lasting relationships. How you listen to other people when they talk about matters of deep concern or things that are distressing is indicative of your listening skills. Listening means paying close attention to what others are saying; beyond that, active listening involves engaging and responding to another person in ways that help you better understand the person's view of the world.

When do you find yourself not listening to others?

_____

_____

_____

_____

When do you find yourself thinking about your response instead of listening to others when they speak?

_____

_____

_____

_____

How can you improve your listening skills?

_____

_____

_____

_____

TIMES I DIDN'T LISTEN

List at least five things that people have asked you to do that you have not followed through on. Then, identify and write down the name of the person who asked you to do these tasks.

WHAT I WAS ASKED TO DO	WHO ASKED ME

ACTIVE LISTENING

Active listening is a learned skill, and results in truly being able to understand the message another person is sending. Active listening involves the following steps:

STEP 1—LISTEN FOR UNDERSTANDING. Change the way you listen: rather than thinking about what you are going to say next when someone is speaking, listen intently for understanding. Make it your priority to discover what the other person is thinking and feeling as they relay their experiences to you.

STEP 2—CLEAR YOUR MIND. Allow your mind to be clear and quiet. Simply enjoy being with the other person and soak in what they are telling you. Allow your mind to listen for the thoughts and emotions hidden beneath the words of the speaker. Prompt the other person to continue talking by using such encouragers as, "Tell me more . . ." or by saying things like, "Uh-huh," or, "I see."

STEP 3—ACT LIKE A MIRROR. Reflect back to the person your understanding of his or her thoughts and feelings. In your own words, restate what you understand the person to be saying while highlighting the emotions that you become aware of.

STEP 4—ASK FOR MORE. Invite the speaker to tell you more if you need additional information or do not understand.

Statements such as, "Can you give me an example of what you just said?" or, "What happened next?" show that you are actively listening to the other person. Remember: Active Listening does not include making judgments or giving advice.

ACTIVE LISTENING EXERCISE

In the following table, I've provided examples of possible exchanges you might have with another person. Use the active listening skills you have learned to show the speaker that you understand him or her. (The first one has been completed as a demonstration.)

WHAT IS SAID	ACTIVE LISTENING RESPONSES
"I am going to my mother's house next weekend, but I'm not sure I want to go!"	"You sound like you're scared of your mother." "You sound really anxious about having to go back and visit your mother." "You're worried about your upcoming visit."
"I get tired of getting beat up every day, but I do not know what to do to stop it!"	

WHAT IS SAID	ACTIVE LISTENING RESPONSES
"You are the worst friend I have ever had. I'm glad you're leaving."	
"I don't understand why grades are so important in school."	
"I was supposed to meet my husband for dinner tonight but my boss asked me to work late. I don't know what to do."	
"I had a great time last night. I would like to do it again."	
"I'm not sure I'm going to be able to do this job. It's fairly complicated and may be too much for me."	
"I seem to always be arguing with my father, but I don't know what to do . . . he's my father and I love him!"	

COMMUNICATING FEELINGS

This category relates to how well you give feedback to other people. People who score high on this scale are able to effectively express their thoughts and feelings to others, in so doing strengthening their relationships. They are able to get across a clear purpose in their communications, express their feelings honestly, and take responsibility for their verbal exchanges.

In what situations do you find yourself unable to say what you feel?

_____
_____
_____
_____

Why are you unable to express yourself in these situations?

_____
_____
_____
_____

How do you feel when you are unable to express your feelings and thoughts to others?

_____
_____
_____
_____

SENDING EFFECTIVE MESSAGES

Sending effective messages is a skill that you can learn. In fact, there are a variety of ways to ensure that your messages will be understood by others. The following five tips will help you communicate more effectively.

Own Your Messages

When sending messages to others, use words such as *I*, *me*, and *my* to communicate your message. By using personal pronouns such as *I*, you let other people know your exact thoughts and feelings. By contrast, when you use phrases like *They said*, it appears as if what you are saying is simply repeating the thoughts and feelings of other people.

For example, if a person says "Some people think that job is too hard," it sounds like he or she is just relaying secondhand information from unknown sources. But if the person says "I think that job sounds awfully hard," the message is more personal.

By using this tactic, you "own" your messages to other people. Words or phrases like *they* or *some people* are ineffective ways to communicate to others. Speak for yourself!

Address the Other Person Directly

Look at the person, speak to him or her directly, and don't repress your feelings. Unexpressed feelings have a tendency to blow up into larger conflicts.

Describe the Actions You Would Like to Address

Describe the behavior or behaviors of the person that you would like to address. These behaviors may include things like not cleaning his or her room, not feeding the dog, staying out too late, or drinking too much.

Express Your Feelings

Express your feelings to others using "I" statements; for example, "I feel angry when you don't pick me up on time," or, "I get upset when you break your word." In the following boxes, practice expressing your feelings to some of your significant others:

SIGNIFICANT OTHER	EXPRESS YOUR FEELINGS

Give Feedback to Others

Be generous in the amount and types of feedback that you give to others. Don't allow positive feelings and thoughts to go unexpressed—verbalizing them can increase the quality of your relationships. In the following boxes, practice expressing positive thoughts and feelings to your significant others:

SIGNIFICANT OTHER	EXPRESS POSITIVE FEEDBACK

NONVERBAL COMMUNICATION

This section relates to your nonverbal communication skills. People who score high on the Communicating Feelings scale are able to convey messages without using words. For example, they communicate by using body actions such as slamming a door or frowning at someone, making eye contact, or by using hand gestures or facial expressions. On the other side of the coin, nonverbal communication skills can also involve sending other people messages of acceptance.

How has your family influenced your nonverbal communication skills?

_____

_____

_____

_____

Was this a positive or negative influence? Why?

_____

_____

_____

_____

In what ways are you aware of how your body language communicates things to other people?

_____

_____

_____

_____

BODY LANGUAGE

Think back to a situation when you were engaged in a stimulating conversation with someone you liked and respected.
How did your body language show the other person your
admiration and your interest in the conversation?

_____

_____

_____

_____

Think back to a situation when you were engaged in a boring,
uninteresting conversation with someone you neither liked
nor respected. How did your body language show the other
person that you were rejecting him or her and uninterested in
the conversation?

_____

_____

_____

_____

How can you start to improve your verbal communication
through your body language?

_____

_____

_____
_____

_____

SHOWING BODY LANGUAGE

Think about your friends. How have you nonverbally shown them that you cared for them?

PERSON	HOW I NONVERBALLY COMMUNICATED WITH HIM OR HER

VALUING DIVERSITY

Diversity among your peers, colleagues, classmates, neighbors, and friends is inevitable in life. It is important that you learn to effectively interact with people from various cultures, social classes, and ethnic groups. You must be able to communicate effectively with a mixed group of people if you are to be successful in your career and life. To begin with, you need to become more aware of your own stereotypes. Complete the table that follows to explore the stereotypes you make:

MY STEREOTYPES

GROUPS	MY STEREOTYPES ABOUT THE GROUP
Males	
Females	
People twenty years older than me	
People twenty years younger than me	
African Americans	
European Americans	
Hispanic Americans	
Asian Americans	
Native Americans	

Teenagers	
Children	
Babies	
People with disabilities	

STEPS TOWARD VALUING DIVERSITY

1. Recognize that diversity exists in the world.

List people you know and then describe how they are different from you.

PEOPLE I KNOW	HOW THEY ARE DIFFERENT FROM ME

2. Find ways to get to know people who are different from you.

PEOPLE WHO ARE DIFFERENT FROM ME	HOW I CAN GET TO KNOW THEM BETTER

3. Build your identity by better understanding your own cultural, ethnic, and religious background.

Describe your cultural background (your sense of your origins):

_____

_____

_____

_____

Describe your ethnic background:

_____

_____

_____

_____

Describe your religious background:

_____

_____

_____

_____

How would you describe yourself as a person?

_____

_____

_____

_____

How would others describe you?

_____

_____

_____

_____

4. Appreciate others for who they are

PEOPLE WHO ARE DIFFERENT FROM ME	WHAT I VALUE ABOUT THEM

three

Assertive Behavior

LEARN HOW TO STAND UP FOR YOURSELF

Because society and the world of work are changing so rapidly and becoming increasingly more stressful, people are more often being forced to stand up for their rights and the rights of others—in other words, to be assertive. Nonassertive behavior is passive, weak, and self-sacrificing. In contrast, aggressive behavior is demanding, hostile, and inconsiderate of others. Assertiveness is right in between, and is often defined as effectively expressing your personal feelings and rights. Assertiveness is standing up for your rights while being careful not to infringe on the rights of others. It is expressing your personal wants and needs, following your interests and personal likes, easily giving and accepting compliments, comfortably disagreeing with others, learning to say no when you do not want to do something, and protecting yourself when a situation seems unfair.

How can you be assertive but not aggressive? As you'll see in this section, it's possible to get what you need and desire while not dominating other people. All people have a right to express their feelings, thoughts, and opinions without criticism from others, and deserve to be treated with respect. When is the proper situation to be assertive? All situations, really. Already, you probably are assertive in some scenarios, but not in other ones. The goal of this section is to increase the variety of situations in which you are more assertive.

In any interpersonal situation, you will respond in one of three ways: nonassertively, assertively, or aggressively. The Assertive Behavior Inventory (ABI) helps you to explore which of those three ways you most often behave.

ASSERTIVE BEHAVIOR INVENTORY

The ABI contains thirty-three statements. Read the statements and decide the extent to which each describes you. In each of the choices listed, circle the number of your response on the line to the right of each statement.

4 = VERY MUCH   3 = USUALLY   2 = SOMEWHAT   I = NOT
LIKE ME   LIKE ME   LIKE ME   LIKE ME

In the following example, the circled 4 indicates the statement is very much like the person completing the inventory:

1. I say nothing when I am provoked.   ④ 3   2   1

After you complete the items, you will simply rerecord the numbers you circled on the lines that follow the inventory and add them together to get your sum totals. This is not a test.

Since there are no right or wrong answers, do not spend too much time thinking about your answers. Be sure to respond to every statement.

4 = VERY MUCH LIKE ME	3 = USUALLY LIKE ME	2 = SOMEWHAT LIKE ME	1 = NOT LIKE ME

1. I say nothing when I am provoked.	4	3	2	1
2. I often react aggressively to other people.	4	3	2	1
3. I express my thoughts and feelings directly to others.	4	3	2	1
4. I keep my feelings to myself.	4	3	2	1
5. I do not mind if I hurt other people.	4	3	2	1
6. I am honest with other people.	4	3	2	1
7. I hide my feelings from significant others.	4	3	2	1
8. I express my feelings through insults and put-downs.	4	3	2	1
9. I treat others with respect and dignity.	4	3	2	1
10. I let other people violate my personal rights.	4	3	2	1
11. I can be very sarcastic.	4	3	2	1
12. I do not feel guilty when I act in my own best interest.	4	3	2	1
13. I let others strip me of my dignity.	4	3	2	1
14. I often label other people.	4	3	2	1
15. I stand up for myself without undue anxiety.	4	3	2	1
16. I let others take advantage of me.	4	3	2	1
17. I often treat people disrespectfully.	4	3	2	1
18. I try not to hurt others as I achieve what I want.	4	3	2	1
19. I do things I do not want to do.	4	3	2	1
20. I force others to do things they do not want to do.	4	3	2	1
21. I stick up for others who cannot stick up for themselves.	4	3	2	1
22. I let other people treat me disrespectfully.	4	3	2	1
23. I don't care about the opinions and feelings of others.	4	3	2	1
24. I constantly search for win-win solutions to problems.	4	3	2	1

25. I often think that my ideas are worthless.	4	3	2	1
26. I often bully or intimidate others.	4	3	2	1
27. I often hold my ground and search for working compromises.	4	3	2	1
28. I constantly apologize for my behavior.	4	3	2	1
29. I often try to get people to change their minds.	4	3	2	1
30. I recognize my own and others' rights and responsibilities.	4	3	2	1
31. I often give in to others, then I do not feel good about myself.	4	3	2	1
32. I make others feel guilty to get my way.	4	3	2	1
33. Even when others do not agree with me, they respect my opinion.	4	3	2	1

SCORING DIRECTIONS

The Assertive Behavior Inventory is designed to measure your level of assertiveness. Three areas have been identified to make up the scales for the ABI: Nonassertive, Aggressive, and Assertive. The items that comprise each of the three scales are grouped so that you can explore how assertively you are behaving. To score your Assertive Behavior Scale:

1. Record each of the scores from the previous two pages on the lines below. For example, if you circled the number 4 for item number 1, you would put a 4 on the line above the 1 on the chart below. Do the same for all thirty-three items.

2. Find the sum totals for each of the three rows and put that total on the line to the right.

1	4	7	10	13	16	19	22	25	28	31	NONASSERTIVE TOTAL

2	5	8	11	14	17	20	23	26	29	32	AGGRESSIVE TOTAL

3	6	9	12	15	18	21	24	27	30	33	ASSERTIVE TOTAL

INTERPRETING YOUR SCORES

The scale on which you scored the highest represents your assertiveness style. The remainder of the assessment contains interpretation materials to help determine how assertively you are acting in your life and in your career. The following sections will provide a description of the three behaviors as well as some self-reflective questions to help you become more assertive.

SCALE DESCRIPTIONS

NONASSERTIVE

You express your wants, opinions, and feelings in an indirect manner. You resort to crying, yawning, or getting angry at yourself. You want others to intuitively know what you want to say. Your needs come after the needs of everyone else. You have trouble saying no and asking for what you want. You may have trouble making eye contact with other people. You let other people violate your personal right to be treated with respect and dignity.

AGGRESSIVE

You have no trouble expressing your wants, opinions, and feelings, but often do so at the expense of others. You use sarcasm and put-downs as a way of controlling other people. You like to get your own way and will do anything to do so. You often attempt to hurt others by your verbal and nonverbal communication. You tend to infringe on the rights of others by expressing your feelings indirectly through labels, insults, and hostile statements. You tend to express your thoughts, feelings, and opinions in a way that violates other people's right to be treated with respect and dignity.

ASSERTIVE

You tend to take other people's rights and feelings into account when you express your wants, opinions, and feelings. Because you are able to defend yourself by using many "I" statements, you listen to others and let them know that you understand their point of view. You tend to know what you want and ask for it, and set limits about how you let others treat you. You receive and give compliments easily, and you can respond effectively to criticism from others.

EXERCISES AND ACTIVITIES

In learning to be more assertive, you need to be aware of the following ground rules:

Know the Position of Other Person Involved

Be aware of what the other person is saying to you or asking you to do. Use your active listening skills to make sure that you understand the true meaning of the request or statement. The following are common listening difficulties that might hinder your ability to be assertive.

INADEQUATE LISTENING It's easy to get distracted from what other people are saying. You might get caught up in your own thoughts, be preoccupied by your own issues, not feel well, or be too eager to help the other person. Perhaps the person has a problem very unlike your own, or the social and cultural difference between you and the other person are too great.

List times when you feel you easily get distracted while talking with others:

_____

_____

_____

_____

When do you find yourself unable to listen to others because of the cultural difference between you?

_____

_____

_____

_____

What specific people do you find it hard to listen to?

_____

_____

_____

_____

EVALUATIVE LISTENING Listening with the intent of judging the person can hinder your ability to absorb what they are saying. If you are judging what the person is saying as good or bad, right or wrong, or acceptable or unacceptable, you are not listening with empathy. If possible, it is important to set judgment aside until you can better understand that person, his or her world, and point of view.

List times when you feel you start to be too evaluative while talking with others:

_____

_____

_____

_____

What specific people do find yourself evaluating?

_____

_____

_____

_____

FILTERED LISTENING Through the socialization process, you have acquired a variety of filters by which you listen to yourself, others, and the world in general. The problem is that these filters often introduce various forms of bias into your listening without you even knowing it. The stronger the cultural filter, the stronger the bias. You may be inadvertently listening to some things but not to others.

List times when you find yourself filtering what others are saying:

_____

_____

_____

_____

What specific people do you tend to filter?

_____

_____

_____

_____

DAYDREAMING Everyone's attention wanders from time to time, especially if the situation in question is a very familiar one. But if you find yourself having a harder and harder time listening to someone, it is probably a sign that you are either avoiding the person or certain topics of conversation.

List times when you feel your attention wandering:

_____

_____

_____

_____

When you mind wanders, what specific people are you talking to? Why does it happen?

_____

_____

_____

_____

REHEARSING Any time you ask yourself the question "How should I respond to what this person is saying?" you distract yourself from what the person is trying to communicate. As you get better at active listening, you'll find you do not need to rehearse what you will say to other people—the words will just come naturally. The best approach is to listen intently to what the person is saying, the themes, and core messages related to their words, then allow your intuition to take over and provide you with the appropriate responses.

List times when you find yourself rehearsing what you will say in conversations:

_____

_____

_____

_____

What specific people are you talking with when you find your-self rehearsing your conversation?

_____

_____

_____

Respect the Feelings of Other Parties Involved

Be sure to let go of feelings of anger, blame, self-pity, and the desire to hurt others. Treat the other person as you like to be treated.

In what ways do you try to hurt others with your words when you are communicating?

_____

_____

_____

_____

What are some universal labels that you seem to use when you get angry (examples might include *stupid, sexist, crazy, selfish, lazy, useless, evil*)?

_____

_____

_____

_____

Define the Situation

State the facts of the situation as you see them. Do not be afraid to express your beliefs and opinions.

When do you find yourself bringing up old history rather than talking about the present situation?

_____

_____

_____

_____

In what situations are you afraid to express your beliefs and opinions?

_____

_____

_____

_____

What is it about certain situations that prevent you from expressing the beliefs and opinions you have?

_____

_____

_____

_____

Describe Your Feelings

Share your feelings so that the other person better understands the importance of the issue for you. Your feelings will play a major role in helping you to achieve your goals. Use a lot of "I" statements, express your true feelings, and connect those feelings to the behaviors of the other person.

"You" messages tend to convey blame and accusation. In what types of situations do you find yourself using a lot of "you" statements?

_____

_____

_____

_____

With whom will you start using more "I" statements?

_____

_____

_____

_____

Express Your Desires, Needs, and Wants

In easy-to-understand statements, clearly state your desires, needs, and wants.

Why do you sometimes have a hard time expressing your desires, needs, and wants?

_____

_____

_____

_____

Reinforce Your Statements

Your assertive communication will be more effective if you demonstrate how your ideas will benefit both you and the other person. Never assume that people can read your mind— tell them how you feel, what you like, and what you want in life, and back that up with examples of how things will be better.

Think back to a situation in which you could have been more assertive in reinforcing your statement. What things could you have said so that both parties would benefit?

_____

_____

_____

_____

PRACTICING ASSERTIVE BEHAVIOR

Think about a situation with another person in which you would like to be more assertive. List that situation and then proceed on paper as if you were going to do so.

Situation: _____

Person Involved: _____

Describe the position of other person(s) involved:

_____

_____

_____

_____

Describe the feelings of other parties involved, and remember to respect them:

_____

_____

_____

_____

Define the situation:

_____

_____

_____

_____

Describe your feelings:

_____

_____

_____

_____

Express your wants:

_____

_____

_____

_____

Reinforce your statement:

_____

_____

_____

_____

Assertiveness Training Exercises

How has your assertiveness style caused problems for you . . .
With your friends?

_____
_____
_____
_____

In your social life?

_____
_____
_____
_____

At work?

_____
_____
_____
_____

With your finances?

_____
_____
_____
_____

With your family?

_____

_____

_____

_____

In other ways?

_____

_____

_____

_____

When I am not being assertive, I:

_____

_____

_____

_____

Self-defeating behaviors I exhibit when I am not assertive include:

_____

_____

_____

_____

Assertiveness Life History

Think back on your development through life. For each of the time periods listed below, describe how assertive or non-assertive you were. Doing so will help you identify the experiences and the people who have influenced your assertive behavior patterns:

As a child, I . . .

_____

_____

_____

_____

In elementary school, I . . .

_____

_____

_____

_____

In middle school, I . . .

_____

_____

_____

_____

In high school, I . . .

_____

_____

_____

_____

As an adult, I . . .

_____

_____

_____

_____

When I Was Assertive

Things I liked about myself:

_____

_____

_____

_____

Things I did not like about myself:

_____

_____

_____

_____

Benefits I received from being assertive:

_____

_____

_____

_____

Reasons I stopped being assertive:

_____

_____

_____

_____

What I Want

In order to assert yourself, you must know what you want in life and in your career. You need to establish priorities, to figure out what is worth fighting for, and what to simply walk away from. In each of the boxes below, list your priorities in each of the categories:

MY PRIORITIES

Personal	
Financial	

Career	
Family	
Friends	
Spirituality	
Community	
Other	

Irrational Thoughts and Assertiveness

A lack of assertiveness often stems from irrational thoughts you have about yourself and the way the world operates. The following chart lists ten common irrational thoughts that cause people to be less assertive. Next to each irrational thought, explain the reasons why you have it, if ever.

MY IRRATIONAL THOUGHTS

IRRATIONAL THOUGHTS	WHY I THINK THAT
Don't rock the boat, just go along with the crowd	
You should always put others' needs before your own	
You should never make mistakes	
You should always accommodate others	
You always need to be sensitive to the needs of others	
You should always stay on other people's good sides	
You should respect the view of people in authority	
It is not polite to question the views of others	
You should keep your opinions to yourself	
Asking questions shows your ignorance	

Nonassertive Situations

You need to identify those situations in which you should be more assertive. By becoming more aware of those situations, you can practice your assertiveness training skills. For each of the situations listed below, describe how you show a lack of assertiveness.

NONASSERTIVE AWARENESS

SITUATIONS IN WHICH I LACK ASSERTIVENESS	WHY I AM NONASSERTIVE
Saying no to others	
Asking for favors	
Disagreeing with others' opinions	
Taking charge of a situation	
Social situations	
Asking for something I want	
Stating my opinions	
Asking for help	
Sexual situations	

Asking for time by myself	
Speaking in front of groups	
Others (list them)	

Describe the situation in which you find yourself being the most nonassertive:

_____

_____

_____

_____

People with Whom I Am Nonassertive

You need to identify those people with whom you should be more assertive. By becoming more aware of those people, you can practice your assertiveness training skills. For each of the people listed below, describe how you may show a lack of assertiveness.

PEOPLE AND MY LACK OF ASSERTIVENESS

PEOPLE WITH WHOM I AM NONASSERTIVE	WHY I AM NONASSERTIVE
Mother	
Father	
Significant other	
Co-Workers	
Children	
Sales clerks	
Religious leaders	
Community leaders	
Neighbors	
Large groups	
Supervisors	
Others (list them)	

Describe the person with whom you would like to be much more assertive:

_____

_____

_____

_____

four

Decision Making

DON'T LEAVE YOUR LIFE TO CHANCE

Sometimes, it's useful to think of life as a constant series of decisions. When you do, you'll see that what happens in your life is largely a result of the decisions you have made; therefore, your proficiency in making effective decisions is one of the primary determinants of how successful you will be. The quality of your decisions, then, often determines the type of education you attain, the work you do, the people you meet, and the lifestyle you develop.

Decisions can be as small as what to wear in the morning or what to have for dinner. On the other hand, decisions can also be very critical, such as choosing where to live, what type of job to pursue, whom you should marry, and if and when to have children. What I hope to show you is that decisions are tools people use to create the type of life they desire. By making good decisions, you can move your life closer to your dreams, take charge of your life, and create the results that you desire. The Decision-Making Approach Inventory (DMAI) is designed to help you understand your strategies and approaches to making decisions, and the results those decisions have on your self-esteem and life in general.

DECISION-MAKING APPROACH INVENTORY

The DMAI assessment contains sixty words that are related to how you make decisions in your life and your career. Read each of the words and decide whether or not the word describes you when you are making decisions. If the statement *does* describe you, circle the word in the column. If the statement *does not* describe you, do not circle it; simply move to the next word.

In the following example, the circled words indicate that they are descriptive of the person completing the inventory.

In Making Decisions in My Life, I Am:

Spontaneous
(Playful)
Optimistic
Undisciplined
(Forgetful)

The Decision-Making Approach Inventory is designed to measure your strength as a decision maker. Take your time responding, but be sure to respond to every word listed. This is not a test, so there are no right or wrong answers.

IN MAKING DECISIONS IN MY LIFE, I AM:

Spontaneous	Adventuresome	Analytical	Reluctant
Playful	Persuasive	Persistent	Fearful
Optimistic	Strong-willed	Self-sacrificing	Submissive
Undisciplined	Competitive	Considerate	Reserved
Forgetful	Resourceful	Respectful	Patient
Unpredictable	Self-reliant	Sensitive	Shy
Haphazard	Strong	Planning	Diplomatic
Disorganized	Forceful	Orderly	Friendly
Inspiring	Independent	Detailed	Consistent
Talkative	Decisive	Idealistic	Slow
Spirited	Confident	Loyal	Reluctant
Cheerful	Domineering	Insecure	Indecisive
Emotional	Rash	Sensitive	Obliging
Enthusiastic	Daring	Pessimistic	Adaptable
Creative	Sure	Perfectionistic	Contented
I. TOTAL ____	**II. TOTAL** ____	**III. TOTAL** ____	**IV. TOTAL** ____
CREATIVE	**INDEPENDENT**	**ANALYTICAL**	**DIPLOMATIC**

SCORING DIRECTIONS

Count the total number of words you circled in each column. Put that column total on the line marked "Total" at the end of the section and then transfer your totals to the space below:

Creative = _____

Independent = _____

Analytical = _____
Diplomatic = _____

    The scale on which you scored the highest is indicative of your decision-making style. If you scored the same on several scales, read about all scales for more information.

    The exercises that follow are designed to help you increase your understanding of the decision-making process. Please read the information that follows about decision making and complete any exercises that are included.

SCALE DESCRIPTIONS

SCALE I: A CREATIVE DECISION-MAKING APPROACH is one in which you rely on "gut-level" reactions. You tend to rely on your internal signals and base your decisions on what feels good to you at the time. You can be somewhat impulsive in making important decisions and sometimes make spontaneous decisions at an unconscious level. You spend little time gathering data, weighing alternatives, and planning, often making decisions based on hunches. This style can be useful when factual data is not available. You have to be careful, however, not to substitute using your intuition for gathering needed information. If this is your style:

List times when this decision-making style has worked well for you:

_____

_____

_____

_____

List times when this decision-making style has not worked
well for you:

_____

_____

_____

_____

Compare and contrast situations in which this creative style
has and has not worked well. What do you notice?

_____

_____

_____

_____

SCALE II: AN INDEPENDENT DECISION-MAKING APPROACH
is one in which you are self-disciplined and determined to
make the right decision. You are very confident in your decision-making abilities and identify and pursue alternatives
quite aggressively. Your singleness of purpose often results in
making the most effective and efficient decision for you. You
tend to make practical decisions that have the most utilitarian
results. You are a forceful leader and other people look to you
to make choices. You are good in emergencies because you can
make decisions quickly and boldly. You are resourceful and

self-reliant in situations where you must make difficult decisions. If this is your style:

List times when this decision-making style has worked well for you:

_____

_____

_____

_____

List times when this decision-making style has not worked well for you:

_____

_____

_____

_____

Compare and contrast situations in which the independent style has and has not worked well. What do you notice?

_____

_____

_____

_____

SCALE III: AN ANALYTICAL DECISION-MAKING APPROACH involves the exploration of your needs and your environment. In this approach to decision making, you identify the decision to be made, weigh all of the various alternatives, and make a logical decision based on information. You weigh the internal and external demands of each situation and compare that data to the benefits and drawbacks of the various alternatives. You gather and consider additional information about alternatives and the possible consequences of each one. You explore alternatives in terms of consequences for both yourself and your environment. The decisions you make tend to fit your needs and your lifestyle. On the other hand, you can take so much time in gathering information that you miss the opportunity to make a decision. If this is your style:

List times when this decision-making style has worked well for you:

_____
_____
_____
_____

List times when this decision-making style has not worked well for you:

_____
_____
_____
_____

Compare and contrast situations in which the analytical style has and has not worked well. What do you notice?

_____

_____

_____

_____

SCALE IV: A DIPLOMATIC DECISION-MAKING APPROACH is one in which you know you should try to gather information about a decision, but you put it off until a later time. You are aware that you should be working to make a decision, but you tend to have trouble "getting in the mood." You have difficulty making up your mind, and often simply don't decide anything. You hesitate to make important decisions and avoid making choices on your own. You tend to fear what others will think about you and/or the decisions you make. In addition, you may be afraid that you will make the wrong decision. If this is your style:

List times when this decision-making style has worked well for you:

_____

_____

_____

_____

List times when this decision-making style has not worked well for you:

_____

_____

_____

_____

Compare and contrast situations in which your style has and has not worked well. What do you notice?

_____

_____

_____

_____

EXERCISES AND ACTIVITIES

The decision-making process usually requires that you consider what you know about a situation, gather information related to that situation and possible alternatives from which to choose, and develop a strategy for making the best decision possible. The following is an example of an effective decision-making process:

Step 1—Recognize that there is a decision to be made. You need to clearly define the nature of the decision you must make. For example: *Should I take a job and relocate to another part of the country?*

Step 2—Gather the relevant information you need to make an effective and timely decision. This information may come from self-analysis, other people, or external resources such as books and videos. For example: *The new job would pay me an additional $10,000. However, I think that the cost of living in that part of the country will be a little more expensive. My spouse would have to give up his job, and he really likes it. I like my current job and may not like the new job. My spouse says he is willing to relocate if I wanted to, but I would be moving farther away from friends and family.*

Step 3—Identify alternatives or paths of action to take based on the information that you have gathered. List all possible and desirable alternatives.

Alternative #1: *I could take the job, relocate without my spouse, and have a long-distance marriage.*

Alternative #2: *I could stay at my current job and turn down the offer for the new job.*

Alternative #3: *I could take the job and ask my spouse to relocate with me.*

Alternative #4: *I could ask my boss for a raise.*

Alternative #5: *I could pass on this opportunity and wait for another job opportunity to come along that is in a more desirable part of the country.*

Step 4—Weigh each alternative based on the information you have already gathered. You should prioritize each of the alternatives based on the most desirable outcomes for each alternative. In our example, the decision maker prioritizes the alternative as:

Ranked #1: *I could pass on this opportunity and wait for another job opportunity to come along that is in a more desirable part of the country.*

Ranked #2: *I could take the job and ask my spouse to relocate with me.*

Ranked #3: *I could stay at my current job and turn down the offer for the new job.*

Ranked #4: *I could take the job, relocate without my spouse, and have a long-distance marriage.*

Ranked #5: *I could ask my boss for a raise.*

Step 5—Choose the alternative that provides you with the best possible outcome. In our example, the decision maker decides to pass up this opportunity and wait for another job opportunity to come along in a more desirable part of the country. After all, she decided that she did not dislike her job, and that her husband did like his. She compared the amount of the increase in salary versus the increase in cost of living and decided that her new salary would probably not increase her monthly take-home pay very much.

Step 6—Take action to begin to implement the alternative you chose in the previous step. For example: *I will turn down this opportunity, but remain aware of new opportunities in the future.*

Step 7—Evaluate whether or not your decision has solved the problem you identified in Step 1. If it has, you may choose to stay with this decision. If, on the other hand, it has not, you may need to gather more information and start the process over. In our example, the decision maker is happy with her decision and will evaluate her desire to relocate at a later date.

Now You Try

Identify a major upcoming decision in your life. Complete the following worksheet that will help you learn and apply the decision-making process:

1. What is the decision to be made?

_____

_____

_____

_____

2. List the relevant information you need to gather in order to make an informed decision:

_____

_____

_____

_____

3. Identify possible choices or plans of action:

_____

_____

_____

_____

4. What are the advantages and disadvantages of each choice?

_____

_____

_____

_____

5. Based on the information you have gathered, which choice is best?

_____

_____

_____

_____

6. Develop an action plan to implement your choice:

_____

_____

_____

_____

7. Describe the outcome of your choice:

_____

_____

_____

_____

8. How effective or appropriate was your choice?

_____

_____

_____

_____

Things To Remember

There are several very important points to remember when you are making important decisions:

**1) DECISIONS INVOLVE A CERTAIN AMOUNT OF UNCER-
TAINTY OR RISK, WHICH WILL PROBABLY MAKE YOU
FEEL UNCOMFORTABLE.** Through proper planning and the use of a rational decision-making approach, you can decrease the amount of risk you feel when making decisions. The following exercises are designed to help you explore your risk-taking behaviors, as they relate to decision making.

What types of decision-making risks do you tend to take most often?

_____

_____

_____

_____

What types of decision-making risks do you need to take more often?

_____

_____

_____

_____

Are there decision-making risks you should not continue to take?

_____

_____

_____

_____

Do the decision-making risks you take reflect what matters most to you? What are these things?

_____

_____

_____

_____

Are you taking the amount of decision-making risks you feel you should be taking? Why or why not?

_____

_____

_____

_____

Are you taking too many of the wrong kinds of decision-making risks? Describe these risks:

_____

_____

_____

_____

What types of risks do you tend to avoid? Why?

_____

_____

_____

_____

2) EFFECTIVE DECISION MAKING RELIES ON A COMBINATION OF RATIONAL THINKING AND INTUITIVE THINKING. You should first utilize the rational approach to develop appropriate alternatives for the decision you are facing. Then, you should rely on your intuitions and feelings about which options are best for you.

When you find yourself being rational and analytical when making decisions, what types of decisions are they? Describe the process you use in these situations.

_____

_____

_____

_____

Do you find yourself getting intuitions or hunches about the decisions you make? Do you follow these hunches? Are they right or do they tend to lead you down a wrong path?

_____

_____

_____

_____

What percentage of your decision-making process is rational and how much is intuitive (e.g., 40 percent rational and 60 percent intuitive)? How can you make the process more effective for you?

_____

_____

_____

_____

BECOMING A SKILLFUL DECISION MAKER

Decisions are based on what you know and what you want in life, but decision makers must also learn and apply certain skills. Look back at the really big decisions you have made in the past—perhaps choices about relationships, school(s), or jobs. List those decisions and write down how you approached them. Then list the outcomes of those decisions, as well as the patterns you notice in your approach to decision making.

Decisions I Have Made

Example of a relationship decision: _____

Outcome: _____

What are the reasons you made a good or poor decision?

_____
_____
_____
_____

Example of a work- or job-related decision: _____

Outcome: _____

What are the reasons you made a good or poor decision?

_____
_____
_____
_____

Example of a family-related decision: _____

Outcome: _____

What are the reasons you made a good or poor decision?

_____

_____

_____

_____

Example of an educational decision: _____

Outcome: _____

What are the reasons you made a good or poor decision?

_____

_____

_____

_____

Example of a health-related decision: _____

Outcome: _____

What are the reasons you made a good or poor decision?

_____

_____

_____

_____

Example of a spiritual/religious decision: _____

Outcome: _____

What are the reasons you made a good or poor decision?

_____
_____
_____
_____

Example of a community-oriented decision: _____

Outcome: _____

What are the reasons you made a good or poor decision?

_____
_____
_____
_____

Review each of your examples, and identify any patterns you notice about your decision-making proficiency:

five

Leisure Time

DO YOU KNOW HOW TO UNWIND?

How do you define leisure? Doing things just for the sake of doing them? Engaging in hobbies? Unproductive or "wasted" time? All of the above? In reality, leisure is much more than time for goofing off. Leisure provides a great many benefits, including a respite from work responsibilities and stress, a way to enjoy life's simple pleasures, enhanced self-esteem, increased relaxation and rest, and a greater sense of belonging. Engaging in constructive leisure activities is a very important component of your ability to maintain your physical health, mental health, and general well-being.

Some people feel guilty when they are engaging in leisure activities, feeling instead they should be working or doing something more productive. These people represent the traditional "work ethic" notion that ties all value to work and productivity. But when we consider all of the benefits that leisure-time activities provide, if becomes clear that we all should strive to achieve a better balance between work and leisure in order to find greater joy and self-fulfillment, manage stress, achieve a balanced lifestyle, and increase overall life satisfaction.

Many people are not able to engage in satisfying leisure activities because they face certain barriers to leisure participation. The Leisure Time Inventory (LTI) will help you to identify your leisure participation barriers and find ways to overcome those obstacles.

LEISURE TIME INVENTORY

The LTI can help you identify the things that stand in the way of your participating in your favorite leisure activities. This assessment contains twenty-five statements divided into five categories. Read each of the statements and decide whether or not the statement describes you. If the statement is very descriptive of your habits, circle the *3* next to that item. If the statement somewhat describes your lifestyle, circle the *2* next to that item. If the statement does not fit your thinking and actions, circle the *1* next to that item.

In the following example, the circled *2* indicates the statement is **Somewhat Descriptive** of the person completing the inventory.

	VERY DESCRIPTIVE	SOMEWHAT DESCRIPTIVE	NOT DESCRIPTIVE
1. I do not have enough money to engage in my favorite leisure activities.	3	②	1

At the end of each category you will add up your total points from the scales and write the sum in the "Total" line provided. Remember, this is not a test. Since there are no right or wrong answers, do not spend too much time on each statement; but be sure to respond to each one.

	VERY DESCRIPTIVE	SOMEWHAT DESCRIPTIVE	NOT DESCRIPTIVE
I. MONEY			
1) I do not have enough money to engage in my favorite leisure activities.	3	2	1
2) The cost (i.e., dues, equipment, etc.) of activities prohibits me from engaging in leisure interests.	3	2	1
3) I must always make sure I have enough money to pay for my leisure activities.	3	2	1
4) I wish I had more money to engage in my favorite leisure activities.	3	2	1
5) I feel bad when a lack of funds prevents me from engaging in an activity.	3	2	1

MONEY TOTAL = _____

	VERY DESCRIPTIVE	SOMEWHAT DESCRIPTIVE	NOT DESCRIPTIVE
II. FREE TIME			
1) My favorite leisure activities are too time-consuming.	3	2	1
2) I do not have the time to pursue my leisure interests.	3	2	1
3) I am not able to experience my leisure interests as frequently as I would like.	3	2	1
4) I often waste time and miss out on opportunities to pursue my leisure interests.	3	2	1
5) I do not always take advantage of the time I do have to pursue my leisure interests.	3	2	1

FREE TIME TOTAL = _____

	VERY DESCRIPTIVE	SOMEWHAT DESCRIPTIVE	NOT DESCRIPTIVE
III. AVAILABILITY			
1) I do not have adequate transportation to participate in my favorite leisure activities.	3	2	1
2) My leisure interests are not provided in the community.	3	2	1

	VERY DESCRIPTIVE	SOMEWHAT DESCRIPTIVE	NOT DESCRIPTIVE
3) My work schedule and other responsibilities prevent me from pursuing my leisure interests.	3	2	1
4) Because of my limited physical mobility, I am restricted from pursuing my leisure interests.	3	2	1
5) Others' negative attitudes about me prevent me from pursuing my leisure interests.	3	2	1

AVAILABILITY TOTAL = _____

	VERY DESCRIPTIVE	SOMEWHAT DESCRIPTIVE	NOT DESCRIPTIVE

IV. HEALTH

1) I am not healthy enough to pursue my favorite leisure interests.	3	2	1
2) My health problems result in pain and discomfort, which prevent me from pursuing my favorite leisure interests.	3	2	1
3) My current medications make it impossible for me to pursue my favorite leisure interests.	3	2	1
4) I feel socially isolated due to my health problems.	3	2	1
5) I am not physically fit enough to engage in my favorite leisure interests.	3	2	1

HEALTH TOTAL = _____

	VERY DESCRIPTIVE	SOMEWHAT DESCRIPTIVE	NOT DESCRIPTIVE
V. LACK OF SKILLS			
1) I do not possess the skills needed to participate in my favorite leisure activities.	3	2	1
2) I will never be able to acquire the needed skills despite my best efforts.	3	2	1
3) I have been asked to participate in leisure activities, but was not able to because of a lack of skills.	3	2	1
4) My favorite leisure activities require certain skills for participation.	3	2	1
5) I do not have the skills required for many leisure activities, but I am willing to work hard and acquire the needed skills.	3	2	1

LACK OF SKILLS TOTAL = _____

SCORING DIRECTIONS

Total the numbers you circled for each of the five sections. Then transfer your totals from each section to the spaces below.

I. MONEY TOTAL   =   _____

II. FREE TIME TOTAL   =   _____

III. AVAILABILITY TOTAL = _____

IV. HEALTH TOTAL = _____

V. LACK OF SKILLS TOTAL = _____

INTERPRETING YOUR SCORES

SCORES FROM 12 TO 15 IN ANY SINGLE AREA ARE HIGH and indicate that you have many barriers to leisure participation and enjoyment in that particular area. You need to make efforts to overcome these barriers.

SCORES FROM 9 TO 11 IN ANY SINGLE AREA ARE AVERAGE and indicate that you have some barriers to leisure participation and enjoyment in that area, but that you are making efforts to continue to find and enjoy leisure activities.

SCORES FROM 5 TO 8 IN ANY SINGLE AREA ARE LOW and indicate that you do not have many barriers to leisure participation and enjoyment.

The first step in effectively dealing with leisure barriers is to recognize that you have them. This awareness will help you to overcome them. Barriers happen for many different reasons—even when you want to do something, there may be circumstances that prevent you from participating. The barriers listed in this section are some of the most common.

For each of the five barriers, answer the journal questions to gain more insight into how you could overcome the barrier and begin enjoying constructive leisure activities.

SCALE DESCRIPTIONS

BARRIER I: MONEY

The lack of money can be a barrier to your leisure participation. You lack the resources required to participate in and enjoy your leisure interests.

How has the lack of money stopped you from engaging in leisure activities?

_____

_____

_____

_____

What leisure activities do you enjoy that you cannot afford?

_____

_____

_____

_____

How do you feel when the lack of funds prevents you from engaging in leisure activities?

_____

_____

_____

_____

Brainstorm some possible ways to earn more money or reduce the costs involved in engaging in your favorite leisure activities:

_____

_____

_____

_____

_____

_____

_____

_____

_____

_____

_____

BARRIER II: FREE TIME

The lack of free time is a barrier to your leisure participation. You may not manage your time well, and what time you do have, you may spend on other activities that do not provide you with sufficient satisfaction. You may even feel that you are wasting time and missing out on satisfying leisure events.

Do you often have trouble finding the time to engage in your favorite leisure activities? If so, why does this happen?

_____

_____

_____

_____

Have you mismanaged your time in the past? If so, how?

_____

_____

_____

_____

Why do you think you have mismanaged your time?

_____

_____

_____

_____

What types of things can you do to free up more time to engage in your favorite leisure activities?

_____

_____

_____

_____

BARRIER III: AVAILABILITY

The lack of availability of your favorite activities is a barrier to your leisure participation. There are times when you would like to participate in a leisure activity but cannot because you do not have adequate transportation, the activity or program is not available in your community, or your work schedule interferes. There may even be physical barriers that prevent you from engaging in your favorite leisure activities.

What types of activities are unavailable to you?

_____

_____

_____

_____

Why are these activities unavailable to you?

_____

_____

_____

_____

How do you feel when you want to engage in an activity but cannot participate because it's not available to you?

_____

_____

_____

_____

What types of things could you do to ensure that you can begin engaging in your favorite leisure activities?

_____

_____

_____

_____

BARRIER IV: HEALTH

Your health is a barrier to your leisure participation. You may be experiencing poor health, or have limited physical or mental abilities due to barriers such as emphysema, complications from medications you are taking, physical disabilities, or pain. These types of barriers prevent you from concentrating on and/or participating in recreational activities.

Have there been times in your life when your health has prevented you from engaging in leisure activities?

_____

_____

_____

_____

What activities have you been unable to enjoy due to problems with your health?

_____

_____

_____

_____

What health barriers have you had in the past? Which barriers do you still have today?

_____

_____

_____

_____

BARRIER V: LACK OF SKILLS

The lack of skills is a barrier to your leisure participation. There will be times when it is possible to acquire the skills that are needed; there will be other times, however, that you will be unable to acquire the skills needed for a particular activity. In those cases, the absence of skills becomes a barrier to your leisure involvement and enjoyment.

Have there been times when you wanted to participate in leisure activities but were unable to due to a lack of skills?

_____

_____

_____

_____

What attempts have you made to attain the needed skills for participation in your favorite leisure activities?

_____

_____

_____

_____

How do you feel when the absence of skills limits your participation in leisure activities?

_____

_____

_____

_____

EXERCISES AND ACTIVITIES

After you have identified your barriers to leisure participation, you must then take action to eliminate or reduce them.

Barrier I: Money

Identify leisure activities that are free to participants. Check out your county's Department of Parks and Recreation, local community centers, and state parks. You should also identify sources to help you find activities that are free or that cost very little: For example, some colleges provide leisure activities to people in the community, usually for a small charge. Realize that you may also have to save and budget your money in order to engage in your favorite leisure activities.

On the following page, list some of the places you can find that are offering free or relatively cheap leisure activities and what those activities are:

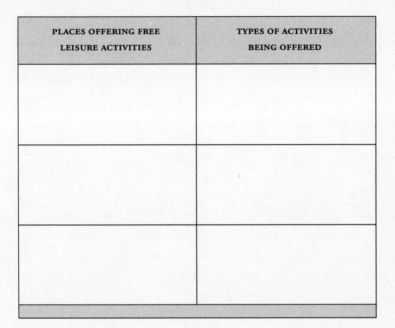

PLACES OFFERING FREE LEISURE ACTIVITIES	TYPES OF ACTIVITIES BEING OFFERED

Barrier II: Free Time

You may need to develop more effective time management skills. It's possible that you're wasting a great deal of time over the course of your day and week. Try to develop a logical system in which you prioritize your activities and chart your responsibilities. Be sure to include free time for leisure activities in your time management system. On the following page, list five ways you waste time, and how you can better manage your schedule.

HOW I WASTE TIME	WAYS TO BETTER MANAGE MY TIME

Barrier III: Availability

Find ways to overcome transportational and other similar types of barriers. Look for leisure activities that can be enjoyed within your home or neighborhood. You might even find ways to use your yard as a leisure facility. Explore the possibility of carpools with other people interested in the same types of leisure activities. Use the Internet to explore and research local groups and organizations that might be starting activities in your community. You might also think about ways to start your own leisure group. Below, list five availability barriers to your favorite leisure activities, and your ideas for how you can overcome them.

BARRIERS TO MY FAVORITE LEISURE ACTIVITIES	HOW I CAN OVERCOME AVAILABILITY BARRIERS

Barrier IV: Health

Learning to cope with limited mental and/or physical abilities is critical. You should realize that you may need to alter your leisure activities to allow for full participation. Don't be afraid to change the rules, if it allows you to take part. Adaptive equipment is often available, as are ramps and lifts that can help meet your needs. Below, list your health barriers to leisure participation, and ideas for how you can overcome them.

HEALTH BARRIERS TO LEISURE PARTICIPATION	HOW I CAN OVERCOME HEALTH BARRIERS

Barrier V: Lack of Skills

There are a variety of strategies you can use to develop the basic skills needed for the leisure activities you're interested in. You can learn from videotapes, the Internet, peers with specific skills, or private instruction. Remember that you'll probably be able to pick up some skills while you're engaging in the activity. Below, list the leisure-based skills you lack, and ideas for how you can gain the skills you need.

LEISURE-BASED SKILLS I LACK	HOW I CAN GAIN LEISURE-BASED SKILLS

Strategies For Overcoming Barriers

In the spaces below, list strategies you will use to overcome your barriers to leisure participation:

LEISURE BARRIER SCALES	STRATEGIES
Money	
Free Time	
Availability	
Health	
Lack of Skills	

six

Money Management

MAKING THE MOST OF YOUR DOLLARS

We tend to have a lot of different emotions about money; we love it, worship it, fear it, hate it, don't understand it, or simply accept it for what it is. People want to live better lives, but often have trouble managing the money they earn. Managing your money and developing a financial plan can be very difficult if you do not understand your money management style. When you are better aware of your personal characteristics as they relate to your money management style, you will be better able to use your money to the fullest and develop a financial plan that fits your personality.

Your personal money management style—how you handle money on a day-to-day basis—will be based on several factors: your fears about spending and running out of money, goals for financial independence, childhood upbringing about money issues, educational level, and emotions related to spending and saving money. The Money Management Style Inventory (MMSI) will help you to identify your money management style and then help you to explore the origins, strengths, and weaknesses of the style.

MONEY MANAGEMENT STYLE INVENTORY

This inventory contains fifty statements. Read each of the statements and decide whether the statement describes you or not. If the statement does describe you, circle the words *Like Me*. If on the other hand, the statement does not describe you, circle the words *Not Like Me*.

In the following example, the circled "Like Me" indicates that the statement describes the person taking the assessment:

I buy whatever brings me pleasure.	(Like me)	Not Like Me

By counting the number of "Like Me" responses you circled in each of the five sections, you will be able to determine your specific money management style. Remember, this is not a test. Since there are no right or wrong answers, do not spend too much time thinking about your answers. Be sure to respond to every statement.

STYLE 1: SPENDERS

I buy whatever brings me pleasure.	Like Me	Not Like Me
I often buy gifts for other people.	Like Me	Not Like Me
I have a hard time budgeting my money.	Like Me	Not Like Me
It is difficult for me to save money.	Like Me	Not Like Me
I buy things on impulse.	Like Me	Not Like Me

I often overspend the money I earn.	Like Me	Not Like Me
I am often in debt.	Like Me	Not Like Me
I am not afraid to spend all the money I have.	Like Me	Not Like Me
No gift is priced too high for me.	Like Me	Not Like Me
I get a thrill from buying things.	Like Me	Not Like Me

TOTAL NUMBER OF "LIKE ME" RESPONSES: _____

STYLE 2: SAVERS

I like to hold on to my money.	Like Me	Not Like Me
I am great at saving money.	Like Me	Not Like Me
I have a budget that I stick to.	Like Me	Not Like Me
I will not buy nonessential items.	Like Me	Not Like Me
I only buy what I need.	Like Me	Not Like Me
I am focused on financial stability.	Like Me	Not Like Me
I like the security of having money in the bank.	Like Me	Not Like Me
I usually pay cash for my purchases.	Like Me	Not Like Me
I am rarely in credit card debt.	Like Me	Not Like Me
I save at least 10 percent of my salary on a monthly basis.	Like Me	Not Like Me

TOTAL NUMBER OF "LIKE ME" RESPONSES: _____

STYLE 3: HOARDERS

I often worry about my finances.	Like Me	Not Like Me
I feel like it is up to me to control my money.	Like Me	Not Like Me
I check my financial account balances often.	Like Me	Not Like Me
I often think about what might happen to my money.	Like Me	Not Like Me

If I just had more money I could stop worrying about it.	Like Me	Not Like Me
I worry that I will not have enough retirement savings.	Like Me	Not Like Me
I like my money in safe investments.	Like Me	Not Like Me
I like to be able to get my hands on my money easily.	Like Me	Not Like Me
I worry when I make a major purchase.	Like Me	Not Like Me
I spend a lot of emotional energy worrying about finances.	Like Me	Not Like Me

TOTAL NUMBER OF "LIKE ME" RESPONSES: _____

STYLE 4: AMASSERS

I want to achieve great wealth.	Like Me	Not Like Me
I believe that along with wealth comes power and status.	Like Me	Not Like Me
I put a lot of time in to managing my money.	Like Me	Not Like Me
I often spend hours hunting for the best investments.	Like Me	Not Like Me
I use a personal finance computer program.	Like Me	Not Like Me
I like to occasionally flaunt my wealth.	Like Me	Not Like Me
I think that having a lot of money impresses people.	Like Me	Not Like Me
I get obsessed with tracking my money.	Like Me	Not Like Me
My self-worth comes from my investment portfolio.	Like Me	Not Like Me
I often shift investments to get the best returns.	Like Me	Not Like Me

TOTAL NUMBER OF "LIKE ME" RESPONSES: _____

STYLE 5: RISK TAKERS

I enjoy taking risks with money.	Like Me	Not Like Me
I am competitive when it comes to money.	Like Me	Not Like Me
I get a rush from intense experience.	Like Me	Not Like Me
I like the adrenaline rush from risking my money.	Like Me	Not Like Me
I try to make a lot of money by playing the lottery.	Like Me	Not Like Me
I thrive on uncertainty.	Like Me	Not Like Me
I always go for broke with my money.	Like Me	Not Like Me
Others say I am too aggressive in my investments.	Like Me	Not Like Me
If I lose money, I believe more will come my way.	Like Me	Not Like Me
I am motivated by variety and change.	Like Me	Not Like Me

TOTAL NUMBER OF "LIKE ME" RESPONSES: _____

SCORING DIRECTIONS

Write your scores to the five sections listed below:

Style 1: Spenders Total =   _____

Style 2: Savers Total =   _____

Style 3: Hoarders Total =   _____

Style 4: Amassers Total =   _____

Style 5: Risk Takers Total = _____

INTERPRETING YOUR SCORES

The area in which you scored the highest tends to be your dominant money management style. Similarly, the area in which you scored the lowest tends to be your least preferred style for managing your money. You should first turn to the section that describes your preferred style. If time permits, you can read about the other money management styles. If you have the same score for several of the styles, you should read each analysis and decide which money management style fits you most. Then you can think of how you combine the two styles.

SCALE DESCRIPTIONS

STYLE 1: SPENDERS

As a Spender, you tend to get carried away by instant gratification in your life. You often feel compelled to spend money or charge purchases very easily and quickly, even if you can't afford them. You will shop and spend compulsively. You often find it difficult to think about anything else other than shopping. Shopping provides you with psychological comfort—you tend to buy things you do not even need, but it is the act of shopping and spending money that satisfies your cravings. You tend to have many credit cards, and many of them are probably charged to their limit. You probably feel like your debts are out of control, but find it difficult to stop the "high" you get from spending money.

Characteristics
- You are prone to frequently getting overdue notices for past-due bills.
- You overspend to feel better about yourself.
- Shopping is a form of addiction for you.
- You often delude yourself about why you keep buying things.
- You feel like you will be happier if you purchase material things.
- You have revolving debt on your credit cards.

What do you think causes you to overspend?

_____

_____

_____

_____

What do you think are the deep-seated roots to your overspending?

_____

_____

_____

_____

How does your financial history affect the way you overspend?

_____

_____

_____

_____

What emotional or psychological voids does spending money fill?

_____

_____

_____

What effect has your childhood and your parents' spending habits had on you?

_____

_____

_____

How does spending money make you feel?

_____

_____

_____

DEVELOP A MONTHLY BUDGET

This worksheet is designed to help you determine the approximate amount of money you are currently spending on a monthly basis:

MONTHLY EXPENSES	CURRENT AMOUNT PAID
Rent or Mortgage	$_____
Car Payment	$_____
TV/Cable	$_____
Loan Repayment	$_____
Medical/Dental Expenses	$_____
Insurance (Life, Auto, Home)	$_____
Medical Insurance	$_____
Credit Card Payments	$_____
Clothing	$_____
Education	$_____
Automobile Expenses	$_____
Parking/Gas	$_____
Food	$_____
Newspaper(s)/Magazines	$_____
Entertainment	$_____
Children's Allowances	$_____
Telephone/Cell Phone	$_____
Gas and Electricity	$_____
Water	$_____
Sewage	$_____
Sanitation	$_____
Household Repairs	$_____
Taxes (State, Local, Federal)	$_____
Child Care	$_____
Other	$_____

TOTAL MONTHLY EXPENSES = $_____

NEEDS VS. WANTS

This exercise is designed to help you separate your needs from
your wants. Complete the sections below by listing what you
think your wants are in the left-hand column and then listing
your needs in the right-hand column. What themes do you see
when you compare the two?

MY WANTS	MY NEEDS

Ways I Can Limit My Spending

In the space below, list some of the things you can do today to begin limiting your overspending. Some suggestions might include cutting up your credit cards, developing a financial plan, seeing a financial planner, and paying off your outstanding debts.

_____

_____

_____

_____

_____

_____

_____

STYLE 2: SAVERS

As a Saver, you tend to be very financially stable. You feel a sense of pride in how you have made and now manage your money. You focus primarily on feeling safe and secure, and doing what you need to do to stay that way. Your debts tend to be under control and all of the choices you make are designed to keep you secure. You frequently check your total assets so that you will feel more psychologically and economically secure.

Characteristics

- When it comes to money you are organized and focused on stability.

- You tend to be educated about money and financial planning strategies.
- You have conservative spending habits.
- You do not like change of any kind.
- You believe that the way to financial security is through steady, conservative investments.
- Regardless of your age, you enjoy planning for your retirement.

How are your money spending and saving habits similar or different from those of your parents?

_____

_____

_____

_____

What would you do if you won $1,000,000 in the lottery? How would you manage the money?

_____

_____

_____

_____

What types of materials do you read about financial planning?

_____

_____

_____

_____

In what ways do you feel you live below your means?

_____

_____

_____

_____

Do your spending and saving habits ever cause conflict between you and significant others? In what ways?

_____

_____

_____

_____

What risk would you like to take with your money that you have been afraid to in the past?

_____

_____

_____

_____

STYLE 3: HOARDERS

As a Hoarder, you tend to believe that the only way to feel financially secure is to hang on to every penny you earn. You tend to continually worry about money, and often let your anxiety get in the way of having fun. You may even feel like a financial disaster is inevitable, and you want to be ready. You prefer thrift over spending and are frugal and do without things you want. You are terribly afraid of losing your money and you want to be prepared for long periods of unemployment or for financial disaster.

Characteristics
- You build a stash of money that you can fall back on in case of an emergency.
- You like budgeting your money and live by a tight monthly budget.
- You like using coupons to save money when you shop.
- You are disciplined about money and are not influenced by advertisements or sales.
- You definitely live within your monetary means.
- You keep a very balanced checkbook.

What risks would you like to begin taking with your money?

_____

_____

_____

_____

How could you better enjoy your money now?

_____

_____

_____

_____

What is your greatest fear related to spending and saving money? Why do you have this fear?

_____

_____

_____

_____

What would being financially comfortable look and feel like to you?

_____

_____

_____

_____

What types of disasters do you fear about money?

_____

_____

_____

_____

Is there a particular incident in your life that made you afraid of losing your money?

_____

_____

_____

_____

In what ways do you think you might be too safe with your money?

_____

_____

_____

_____

Has your life suffered in any way because you will not spend money on things you can afford? List those ways:

_____

_____

_____

_____

STYLE 4: AMASSERS

As an Amasser, money is about status and living as if you make more money than you really do. It is through money that you are able to keep score and compare yourself with others. You like to keep up with and surpass those around you. You feel like the more you have, the more successful you are; therefore, your worth is tied to your possessions. Buying upscale materials and goods provides you with psychological comfort. You may purchase nice cars, homes, and clothes but you probably do not have an emergency fund set aside for a rainy day. You may not even realize how much money you are spending as opposed to saving or investing.

Characteristics
- You have the drive and energy to make a lot of money.
- You are willing to work hard and you take great pride in your accomplishments.
- You are a natural achiever and enjoy spending money as a symbol of your achievements.
- You think that appearances are important, and want everyone to think you have the nicest things.
- You tend to overestimate how much you earn and underestimate how much you spend.
- When you see things you want, you go ahead and buy them regardless of how much they cost.
- You often put yourself in financial jeopardy so that you can purchase upscale possessions.
- You often find yourself driven to purchase things you cannot afford, and any money you save is to make future purchases that will help you appear wealthy.

What drives you to want to amass a lot of money?

_____

_____

_____

_____

How does amassing and spending money symbolize your achievement?

_____

_____

_____

_____

Why are appearances so important to you?

_____

_____

_____

_____

What types of things have you purchased that you could not afford?

_____

_____

_____

_____

DETERMINING YOUR FINANCIAL GOALS

Describe your financial goals for one, five, ten, and twenty years. Be as specific as possible.

One Year	
Five Years	
Ten Years	
Twenty Years	

DETERMINING YOUR PERSONAL GOALS

Remember that your financial goals are related to your personal and family goals. Describe your personal and family goals for one, five, ten, and twenty years. Be as specific as possible. Examples might include identifying a new leisure activity, spending ten more hours a week with your family, and saving for finances to assist your children through college.

One Year	
Five Years	
Ten Years	
Twenty Years	

DETERMINING YOUR BUSINESS EXPECTATION

Because one of the best ways to amass money is through owning your own business, the following questions have been designed to help you explore your entrepreneurial interests.

What type of business would you like to start?

_____

_____

_____

_____

How big do you want your business to be?

_____

_____

_____

_____

How much income do you expect to generate?

_____

_____

_____

_____

How much time do you want to devote to your business?

_____

_____

_____

_____

How will operating a business affect your lifestyle?

_____

_____

_____

_____

What compromises are you willing to make in order to meet your goals?

_____

_____

_____

_____

What need do you expect to fill with your business?

_____

_____

_____

_____

Describe the types of clients/customers you expect to have:

_____

_____

_____

_____

STYLE 5: RISK TAKERS

As a Risk Taker, you tend to get an emotional rush from spending and managing money. You believe that the only way to get what you want in life is to take significant risks. You always want whatever is bigger and better, both in your life and your career. You like to gamble on hunches when it comes to money, and you trust your instincts that your risks will pay off.

Characteristics
- You always go for broke with your money.
- You tend to be charismatic and creative in earning and spending money.

- You don't mind unpredictability and uncertainty when it comes to managing your money.
- You will gamble on your own ability to make a lot of money if something happens to what you have.
- If you do invest your money, you probably will invest in the highest-risk stocks or commodities.

RISK-TAKING BEHAVIOR

The following questions are designed to help you explore your risk-taking money behaviors:

What types of risks do you take with money?

_____

_____

_____

_____

What are you thinking when you take these risks?

_____

_____

_____

_____

Describe the feelings you get when you take money risks:

_____

_____

_____

_____

How does your risk-taking with money affect others?

_____

_____

_____

_____

What do you hope to achieve by taking risks with money?

_____

_____

_____

Describe how you have attempted to "go for broke" with your money risks:

_____

_____

_____

Are you taking too many of the wrong kinds of money risks? Describe these risks:

_____

_____

_____

EXERCISE AND ACTIVITIES

My Money History

Answer the following questions about how money was handled in your family when you were growing up.

In what town and state did you grow up?_____

How did where you grew up affect your money-management style?

_____

_____

_____

_____

How much money did your family have and how has this affected your current thoughts about money?

_____

_____

_____

_____

What were your father's thoughts about money and money management?

_____

_____

_____

_____

Write a statement that summarizes your current risk-taking money behavior:

_____

_____

_____

_____

_____

_____

_____

_____

Next write a statement that describes how you would like to change your risk-taking money behaviors:

_____

_____

_____

_____

_____

_____

_____

_____

What were your mother's thoughts about money and money management?

_____

_____

_____

_____

MONEY MANAGEMENT PRACTICES

How was money handled in your family?

_____

_____

_____

_____

Who took care of the money management process?

_____

_____

_____

_____

Who takes care of money management in your current family?

_____

_____

_____

_____

How can you manage your money more effectively?

_____

_____

_____

_____

seven

Time Management

MANAGE TIME SO IT DOES NOT MANAGE YOU

Time is a valuable resource, but it means different things to different people. For people who are good managers of time, it brings relaxation, satisfaction, and success. These people tend to have productive work habits, effective relationships, and successful lives. For others who are managed *by* time, time brings anxiety, stress, exhaustion, and complication. One of the leading causes of stress is that people have too much to do, and not enough time to do it. In this fast-paced society, learning how to manage your time can help you to alleviate stress and reduce anxiety in your life.

If you are struggling with time management, don't worry—you're not alone. Many people feel the need to learn effective time management skills. But what most people don't know is that the secret to effective time management lies in the identification of your specific time management style. The Time Management Style Inventory (TMSI) can help you identify your specific style. By understanding more about your time management style, you will be better prepared to organize your life and your work, minimize the stress in your life, maximize the results of goals you set for yourself, and enhance how you relate to time.

TIME MANAGEMENT STYLE INVENTORY

The TMSI can help you identify the specific ways in which you manage time in both your personal and professional lives. This assessment contains forty-four statements, divided into four style categories. Read each of the statements and decide how each reflects your style. Using the following descriptors, write the number that represents your choice in the blank space next to each item. For example:

1 = Not Like Me
2 = Somewhat Like Me
3 = Occasionally Like Me
4 = Usually Like Me
5 = Very Much Like Me

1. I am exhausted a lot of the time. _3_
2. I am late a lot of the time.   _4_

In the first example, the *3* means that the test taker feels the statement is "Occasionally Like Me," while in the second example, the *4* means that the test taker feels the statement is "Usually Like Me." Do the same for all forty-four items that follow. Do not think too much about each item; simply write the number that you feel represents how much each statement represents you.

When you are finished, tally the sum totals for each column and fill them in at the end of the inventory.

1 = **Not Like Me**

2 = **Somewhat Like Me**

3 = **Occasionally Like Me**

4 = **Usually Like Me**

5 = **Very Much Like Me**

1. I am exhausted a lot of
   the time.   _____

2. I am late a lot of the time.   _____

3. I have my car serviced at
   the appropriate times.   _____

4. I often put off calling
   people I don't like.   _____

5. I feel driven to accomplish
   more than other people.   _____

6. I never feel like I am
   rushing from one thing
   to another.   _____

7. I keep maps where I can
   get to them easily.   _____

8. I complete most projects
   at the last minute.   _____

9. I feel driven to get more
   money than other people.   _____

10. People say that I "have
    no sense of time."   _____

11. I throw away mail that
    I know is unimportant.   _____

12. I take pride in the fact
    that I usually put things
    off until the last minute.   _____

13. I do most things in
    a hurry.   _____

14. I rarely, if ever, use
    a watch.   _____

15. I have my short-term
    goals written down.   _____

16. I rarely take risks
    because I am afraid of
    making mistakes.   _____

17. I often try to do several
    things at the same time.   _____

18. I have time for hobbies
    or leisure activities.   _____

19. I say no if a commitment
    will take away from
    my personal time.   _____

20. I often overcommit
    myself.   _____

21. I often set and work
    toward unattainable
    goals.   _____

22. I have trouble making
    set deadlines.   _____

23. I usually reconfirm
    appointments I made
    some time ago.   _____

24. I often put things off
    because I am afraid
    of failing.   _____

25. I am competitive and
    always have to win.   _____

26. I will delegate jobs
    I cannot complete.   _____

27. I have a daily planner
    I carry with me.   _____

28. I wait until it is absolutely
    necessary to see a doctor
    or dentist.   _____

29. I have trouble relaxing
    and enjoying myself.   _____

30. Being late does not
    bother me.   _____

31. I make copies of most of
    the documents I sign.   _____

32. I often postpone
    appointments or
    meetings.   _____

33. I often have little time for
    my friends.   _____

34. I rarely worry about
    the future.   _____

35. I have a filing system for
    personal papers.   _____

36. I put off tasks that are not
    clearly defined or planned.   _____

37. I have unrealistic
    expectations of myself.   _____

38. Others believe I have
    a lax attitude.   _____

39. I often write down my
    plans for the future.   _____

40. I put off tasks that seem
    overwhelming to me.   _____

41. I take on more projects
    than I have time
    to complete.   _____

42. I am rarely in a hurry to
    do anything.   _____

43. I try to return phone calls
    and e-mails within
    twenty-four hours.   _____

44. I often put off unpleasant
    tasks.   _____

FINAL TOTALS   _____   _____   _____   _____
                            A   B   C   P

SCORING DIRECTIONS

If you have not already done so, count down each of the four columns and add the numbers you put in each of the blank spaces. Then, put the sum totals for each of the columns in the spaces marked "Final Totals." Then transfer your Final Totals to the section below.

INTERPRETING YOUR SCORES

A (TYPE A) = _____ People scoring highest on the A scale tend to have time management styles that are achievement oriented and driven toward success. You often take on more obligations and commitments than there is time available, and set and strive for high goals. You often have trouble finding time to relax.

B (TYPE B) = _____ People scoring highest on the B scale feel no time urgency. You go with the flow and feel like everything will get done in its own time. You have a limited sense of time and are rarely in a hurry.

C (TYPE C) = _____ People scoring highest on the C scale tend to have time management styles that allow them to make the most of the time they have. You plan for the future and manage your time very well. You are able to balance work and leisure, and get done all you need to get done.

P (PERFECTIONISTIC) = _____ People scoring highest on the P scale are procrastinators. You tend to always put things off until a later time. You often overcommit yourself and then feel overwhelmed and are unable to fulfill your commitments. You will put things off until it is absolutely necessary to attend to them.

Go to the description of the scale(s) on which you scored highest.

SCALE DESCRIPTIONS

TYPE A TIME MANAGEMENT STYLE

People with a Type A Time Management style show a strong sense of time urgency. They tend to take on more commitments and obligations than they have time to complete in order to feel driven. They feel they must accelerate the rate at which they think, plan, and act in all areas of their lives. People with Type A styles tend to speak quickly and do more than one thing at a time, which helps them feel like they can accomplish more in less time. They are very achievement oriented and driven to strive for high goals. They tend to be very competitive in both work and play. Those in this group show intense concentration and alertness while attempting to complete tasks, tend to be somewhat perfectionistic, and rarely let others do tasks that they can complete themselves. They exhibit extreme "all-or-nothing" thinking and rarely see any shades of gray. Type A personalities are preoccupied by "shoulds" and tend to think and say things like, "I should never make mistakes," and, "I should never get sick or tired."

Type A Tendencies
- Being perfectionistic
- Showing excessive thoroughness
- Hoarding material things
- Being defensive
- Showing insecurity
- Being hyperaggressive

- Being too driven
- Being too competitive

MANAGING TYPE A BEHAVIORS

The following exercises and suggestions will help you to manage your Type A Time Management style.

Find a Hobby

What sorts of things could you enjoy that are not work related?

_____

_____

_____

_____

What types of activities can you do that are not competitive in nature?

_____

_____

_____

_____

How and why do you deny yourself the activities you just listed?

_____

_____

_____

_____

What would you like to accomplish within the next five years?

_____

_____

_____

_____

How could you accomplish these things in a more relaxed time frame?

_____

_____

_____

_____

Monitor Negative Self-Talk

What sorts of things do you say to yourself when you start to feel driven to accomplish things?

_____

_____

_____

_____

What "shoulds" do you find yourself thinking, either about yourself or other people?

_____

_____

_____

_____

What could you do to stop being so demanding of yourself and other people?

_____

_____

_____

_____

Activate Your Right-Brain

What types of literature and music do you enjoy, or could you enjoy, without being competitive or obsessed with them? Now, spend some time reading and listening to music simply for the pleasure of doing it!

_____

_____

_____

_____

What types of creative and artistic activities could you engage in that would be solely for the enjoyment of doing them? Now, spend some time being creative simply for the pleasure of doing it!

_____

_____

_____

_____

Look at Previous Relaxation Successes

What types of activities have you enjoyed in the past that were relaxing to you?

_____

_____

_____

_____

Which ones do you want to begin enjoying again?

_____

_____

_____

_____

Schedule Time Each Day to Rest and Relax

List some things you could do each day to slow down or stop your overachieving ways:

_____

_____

_____

_____

What other types of stress-reducing techniques can you begin using to help you relax (meditation, walking, jogging, deep breathing, hobbies)?

_____

_____

_____

_____

Learn to Do Things Just for the Fun of It

What types of activities do you want to do simply because they are fun and not because they will help your career?

_____

_____

_____

_____

What types of commitments and obligations do you take on that you do not need to?

_____

_____

_____

_____

With whom do you have the most fun, and what things do you do?

_____

_____

_____

_____

My Fun Journal

If you were not at work, describe what you would consider a fun day:

_____

_____

_____

_____

_____

_____

_____

_____

TYPE B TIME MANAGEMENT STYLE

People with a Type B Time Management pattern have the capacity to appreciate affection, beauty, aesthetics, nature, and creative novelty. This capacity allows them to revel in a variety of events, like the sunset, children playing, or a flower blooming in their garden. They tend to have the opposite characteristics of the Type A person. Type Bs are very aware of the need to be on time, but they seldom experience time urgency and impatience in activities. They seldom feel compelled to approach every task with a strict time deadline and are rarely in a hurry. People who fall under the Type B category are more patient with others and with themselves, take time for contemplation, and tend to value every moment. They are not compulsively preoccupied with the future but rather just like to live in the moment. Type Bs do not feel the need to control other people and like to just "go with the flow" of life.

Type B Tendencies
- Being very secure
- Being slow to temper
- Reflecting on self
- Being deliberate
- Moving slowly
- Cooperating with others
- Being very patient
- Appreciating themselves
- Putting things off

MANAGING TYPE B BEHAVIORS

The following exercises and suggestions will help you to manage your Type B Time Management style.

Look at Previous Successes

List the previous time management successes you have had:

_____

_____

_____

_____

What things can you do to have more of these successes?

_____

_____

_____

_____

Develop a plan to begin achieving more success:

_____

_____

_____

_____

Set More Achievable Goals

What would you like to accomplish within the next five years?

_____

_____

_____

_____

What would you like to accomplish within the next three years?

_____

_____

_____

What would you like to accomplish within the next year?

_____

_____

_____

_____

What would you like to accomplish within the next three months?

_____

_____

_____

_____

What would you like to achieve within the next three weeks?

_____

_____

_____

_____

Activate Your Left-Brain

How could you be more aggressive in your career development?

_____

_____

_____

_____

Set some goals for enhancing your career:

_____

_____

_____

_____

_____

_____

_____

_____

TYPE C TIME MANAGEMENT STYLE

People with a Type C Time Management style are able to go beyond their usual level of functioning to achieve new heights of personal and professional performance. They are able to perform tasks effortlessly, are optimistic and confident, and always tend to love what they do. Their thoughts and actions always seem to be naturally unified, and they are able to effectively make decisions. Concentration tends to be focused and complete. They are able to easily engage and become fully connected with whatever they are doing. They are alive, energetic, and feel a sense of total joy with the world. Type Cs love a challenge and tend to be confident and in control at all times. People who exhibit this style are calm, able to accomplish a great deal with a minimum of effort.

Type C Tendencies
- Remaining calm regardless of the situation
- Being focused
- Being energized
- Feeling alive
- Taking calculated risks
- Excelling in all they do
- Demonstrating competency
- Having a success-oriented outlook

MANAGING TYPE C BEHAVIORS

The following exercises and suggestions will help you to manage your Type C Time Management style.

Continue to Define Your Role Expectations

List what is expected of you by yourself or by others that is unrealistic.

LOCATION	UNREALISTIC EXPECTATIONS
At Home	
At Work	
With Friends	
At School	
In the Community	
Other	

Continue to Spend Time by Yourself As Well As with Others

How has your family upbringing or ethnic background affected your sense of time?

_____

_____

_____

_____

What could you block out and not do, in order to have more time by yourself?

_____

_____

_____

_____

How can you spend more time with other people?

_____

_____

_____

_____

*Remind Yourself to Say No
to Others if You Mean No*

What types of situations do you find yourself saying yes when you mean no?

_____
_____
_____
_____

Why do you find yourself saying yes in these situations?

_____
_____
_____
_____

To whom do you say yes when you mean no?

_____
_____
_____
_____

To whom do you need to start saying no to more often?

_____
_____
_____
_____

What fears do you have about being more assertive?

_____

_____

_____

_____

Continue to Engage in
Pleasurable Leisure Activities

What are some leisure activities you can engage in to have time
by yourself? Make a schedule of the pleasurable activities you
want to engage in.

PLEASURABLE ACTIVITIES	WHEN I WILL DO THEM EACH DAY/WEEK

Be Assertive When You Need to Be

Following is an example of an unassertive person becoming more assertive with her husband.

What are your rights? What do you want and need?	"I need more affection from my husband."
Plan a time to discuss your problem	Tuesday night after dinner
Define the problem	"I think that we are in a rut! I don't feel like we are as affectionate as we used to be."
Describe the problem using "I" messages	"I feel sad and unloved."
Express your needs	"I need you to show me affection more often."
Express the positive outcome	"It will make our marriage more loving and fulfilling."

NOW YOU TRY IT

List a situation in which you find yourself not being as assertive as you could be. Then write about how you intend to be more assertive.

What are your rights? What do you want and need?	
Plan a time to discuss your problem	
Define the problem	
Describe the problem using "I" messages	
Express your needs	
Express the positive outcome	

TYPE P TIME MANAGEMENT STYLE

People with a Type P, or Perfectionistic, Time Management pattern have extremely demanding expectations of themselves and others. They feel like they always know what is correct and how things should be done. They set standards for themselves that are beyond their reach and impossible to achieve. Since perfectionists measure their worth in terms of accomplishment and productivity, they rarely feel like they are very worthy as human beings, think they must be perfect in all they attempt, and have little tolerance for mistakes in themselves or in others. They feel that if something is done incorrectly it can never be changed. Perfectionists believe that when others do not do what they desire, they are "bad" human beings.

Perfectionistic Tendencies
- Procrastinating
- Being too thorough
- Having unrealistic beliefs
- Being overly defensive
- Being too picky
- Valuing productivity
- Being plagued by "shoulds"
- Being very self-critical
- Being hypercritical of others

MANAGING PERFECTIONISTIC BEHAVIORS

The following exercises and suggestions will help you to manage your Perfectionistic Time Management style.

Stop Procrastinating

What do you find yourself putting off until later?

_____

_____

_____

_____

Why do you put these things off?

_____

_____

_____

_____

What do you gain from procrastinating?

_____

_____

_____

_____

How has procrastinating hurt or helped you?

_____

_____

_____

_____

Monitor Negative Self-Talk

What negative words do you hear that "little voice inside your head" saying to you when you put things off?

_____

_____

_____

_____

How can you stop the little voice inside your head?

_____

_____

_____

_____

Replace "Shoulds" with "Oughts"

What do you feel obligated to do or think that you should always do?

_____

_____

_____

_____

Now make each of the above "shoulds" into "oughts":

_____

_____

_____

_____

Stop Worrying About How Others View You

What do you worry about in trying to impress others?

_____

_____

_____

_____

What do you think others say about you?

_____

_____

_____

_____

How are you critical about yourself?

_____

_____

_____

_____

How does your perfectionism stop you from completing certain tasks?

_____

_____

_____

_____

Stop Overreacting to Mistakes

List possible mistakes, and list the worst things that could happen because of them.

MISTAKE	WHAT IS THE WORST THAT CAN HAPPEN?

EXERCISES AND ACTIVITIES

What is your primary Time Management Type? _____

Which qualities listed for your time management type best describe you?

_____

_____

_____

_____

Which qualities listed for the other time management types would you like to develop?

_____

_____

_____

_____

Which "tendencies" are listed for your time management type that you might like to change or alter?

_____

_____

_____

_____

What could you do now to make specific changes in your time management type?

_____

_____

_____

_____

How could you be better time oriented and balanced?

_____

_____

_____

_____

How can knowledge of your time management style improve your relationships, career success, and educational attainment?

_____

_____

_____

_____

What now do you value most about your specific time management style?

_____

_____

_____

_____

From other people you know who have a different time management style than yours, what types of characteristics would you most like to have?

OTHER PEOPLE I KNOW AND THEIR TIME MANAGEMENT STYLE	CHARACTERISTICS I WOULD LIKE TO HAVE FROM EACH OF THEM

eight

Relationship Quality

RESCUE YOUR RELATIONSHIPS

Relationships are an essential part of growing and becoming an effective adult, and play an important role in your overall success in life. They're critical to your happiness both at work and at home. In the business world, relationships play a major role in your security and productivity, as well as the growth and success of the company for which you work. Successful people will take advantage of every opportunity to acquire information about people and develop effective relationships with them. At home, having an intimate relationship with people you love and who love you can ensure that your emotional, social, and intimacy needs are met. Positive relationships provide you with people who care about you and are willing to help you grow personally, people you can count on when you are in a stressful or fearful situation, and people with whom you can develop both friendships and intimate relationships.

Intimate relationships supply a depth and meaning that few other human experiences provide. Intimate relationships often allow you to transcend daily problems and hassles, and offer you the potential for tremendous satisfaction and enjoyment in life. On the other hand, ineffective or unsatisfying intimate relationships can be one of the greatest sources of pain. The Relationship Quality Inventory (RQI) will help you to examine the quality of your intimate relationships.

RELATIONSHIP QUALITY INVENTORY

This assessment contains thirty-two statements that are related to relationships with a significant other in your life. Read each of the statements and decide whether or not the statement describes you. If the statement is true, circle the number next to that item under the "True" column. If the statement is false, circle the number next to that item under the "False" column.

In the following example, the circled number under "FALSE" indicates the statement is not true for the person completing the inventory.

	TRUE	FALSE
(A) My partner and I fight a lot.	1	②

After you have completed the items, you will be able to determine your scores by simply adding together the numbers you circled for each statement. This is not a test. Since there are no right or wrong answers, do not spend too much time thinking about your answers. Be sure to respond to every statement.

		TRUE	FALSE
(A)	My partner and I rarely argue.	2	1
(A)	Discussions rarely become heated arguments.	2	1
(A)	Nobody ever wins our arguments.	1	2
(A)	Arguments always end up leaving us both feeling worse.	1	2
(A)	My partner and I fight a lot.	1	2
(A)	Our arguments end up in name calling.	1	2
(A)	Personal attacks are not common when we fight.	2	1
(A)	I often feel on guard with my partner.	1	2
(B)	My partner is my best friend.	2	1
(B)	I always have fun when I am with my partner.	2	1
(B)	I am spiritually incompatible with my partner.	1	2
(B)	I love spending time with my partner.	2	1
(B)	My partner and I both have the same values.	2	1
(B)	My partner and I have similar interests.	2	1
(B)	My partner and I do not have the same goals.	1	2
(B)	My partner and I have similar socioeconomic backgrounds.	2	1
(C)	I often think about my partner when we are apart.	2	1
(C)	I find my partner sexy and attractive.	2	1
(C)	I would marry the same person if I had to do it over again.	2	1
(C)	I am not sure my partner appreciates me.	1	2
(C)	Our sex life is fulfilling.	2	1
(C)	I often kiss my partner affectionately.	2	1
(C)	I feel accepted by my partner.	2	1
(C)	I rarely tell my partner "I love you."	1	2
(D)	I am familiar with the stresses of my partner.	2	1
(D)	I know my partner's hopes and aspirations.	2	1

(D) I know my partner's life and career dreams.	2	1
(D) I cannot name my partner's three best friends.	1	2
(D) I know my partner's three favorite movies.	2	1
(D) I know my partner's three greatest fears.	2	1
(D) I do not know who my partner's favorite artist is.	1	2
(D) I know the three most important times in my partner's life.	2	1

SCORING DIRECTIONS

The Relationship Quality Inventory is designed to measure the quality of your intimate relationships. To get your (A) Conflict score, total the numbers you circled for statements marked (A) in the previous section. You will get a score from 8 to 16. Put that number on the line next to the (A) Conflict Total scale that follows. Then, do the same for the other three scales: (B) Compatibility Total, (C) Love Total, and (D) Intimate Knowledge Total.

(A) CONFLICT TOTAL = _____
(B) COMPATIBILITY TOTAL = _____
(C) LOVE TOTAL = _____
(D) INTIMATE KNOWLEDGE TOTAL = _____

Add the four scores you listed above to get your Overall Relationship Quality Total. Total scores on this assessment range from 32 to 64. Put your overall total score in the space below.

OVERALL RELATIONSHIP QUALITY TOTAL = _____

INTERPRETING YOUR SCORES

SCORES FROM 8 TO 10 IN ANY SINGLE AREA, OR A TOTAL FROM 32 TO 42, indicate that you are probably experiencing a lack of relationship quality. A low score suggests that you are experiencing a great deal of conflict, you are not as compatible as you could be, you may have fallen out of love, and are not intimately familiar with your significant other.

SCORES FROM 11 TO 13 IN ANY SINGLE AREA, OR A TOTAL FROM 43 TO 53, indicate that you are probably experiencing average relationship quality. Your score is similar to other people taking the scale. It suggests that you are experiencing some conflict, you tend to be somewhat compatible with each other, you are starting to lose that sense of excitement about your significant other, and you may not truly intimately know your partner.

SCORES FROM 14 TO 16 IN ANY SINGLE AREA, OR A TOTAL FROM 54 TO 64, indicate that you are probably experiencing excellent relationship quality. A high score suggests that you are able to easily resolve conflicts in your intimate relationships, you are compatible in every way with your significant other, you are still very much in love, and you have an intimate knowledge of your partner.

SCALE DESCRIPTIONS

SCALE A: CONFLICT

People scoring low on this scale are experiencing a lot of conflict in their relationship. When two people with unique opinions, values, interests, and personalities are together, conflict will inevitably occur. Some of these conflicts are minor issues, such as what color to paint the living room of your house, while some are much larger issues, such as whether or not to have children. But in effective relationships, couples are able to identify and define areas of disagreement, and then find ways to effectively resolve the conflicts and develop appropriate coping mechanisms.

SCALE B: COMPATIBILITY

People scoring low on this scale are unable to connect with each other because they lack basic compatibility. They find that they are fundamentally very different from each other. In effective relationships, partners are able to connect with each other because they enjoy spending free time together, have fun engaging in activities together, and have the same basic needs, goals, and dreams.

SCALE C: LOVE

People scoring low on this scale often find themselves falling out of love with their partner. If you find yourself thinking about how things used to be in your marriage or relationship, this may be a sign of falling out of love, starting to lose fondness and admiration for each other. In effective relationships, partners exhibit a sense of excitement about one another, maintain a sense of respect for their partner, and find themselves as much in love as the day they fell in love.

SCALE D: INTIMATE KNOWLEDGE

People scoring low on this scale are not intimately familiar with their significant other and his or her world. Sometimes couples fall into the habit of inattention to what has gone on or is currently going on in the life of their partner. In effective relationships, partners truly know one another. They remember the major events in each other's lives, understand each other's hopes and dreams, and relate to each other's most intimate thoughts and feelings.

Stress can manifest itself in a variety of ways in a relationship. Regardless of your score on the RQI, the following exercises have been designed to help you enhance your relationship with your partner. Try doing all of the relationship enhancement techniques that follow, then choose to continue the ones you feel most comfortable doing.

EXERCISES AND ACTIVITIES

Partner Exploration

The more you know about each other's inner worlds, the more profound the relationship between you and your partner will be. Self-exploration and the sharing of your findings with each other will have exciting effects on your relationship.

EXPERIENTIAL EXERCISE—PARTNER EXPLORATION
The following questions are designed to guide you and your partner through the self-exploration process and then to help each of you share this information. Answer the following

questions as truthfully as possible and then discuss your entries with each other.

What has happened in your life that you are the most proud of?

_____

_____

_____

_____

What has happened in your life that you are the least proud of?

_____

_____

_____

_____

How would you describe your childhood to other people?

_____

_____

_____

_____

What difficult events have you gone through in your life?

_____

_____

_____

_____

Describe any traumas or emotional difficulties you encountered during your childhood:

_____

_____

_____

_____

If you had the chance, how would you have changed your life?

_____

_____

_____

_____

What decisions have you made that you are most proud of, and least proud of?

_____

_____

_____

_____

How would you like to be remembered when you die?

_____

_____

_____

_____

Describe your career dreams:

_____

_____

_____

_____

What would you most like to change about yourself?

_____

_____

_____

_____

What differences exist between you and your partner when it comes to expressing emotions?

_____

_____

_____

_____

Mindfulness

Mindfulness is that state in which you are fully in touch with the present moment, so that you can see its fullness, hold it in your awareness, and come to know and understand it entirely. It is being aware of what you and your partner are doing at the time, and viewing the event in a nonjudgmental way. The type of attention associated with mindfulness increases your awareness and clarity, and allows you to accept the reality of the present moment. When you lose awareness of the present moment, you create problems for yourself because you are forced to rely on unconscious and automatic thoughts and behaviors that have developed over the years.

Mindfulness is more difficult than it sounds. Many forces work against you being mindful during any activity. Some of these forces are the creation of your own mind and include the labels you attach to your performance, rehearsing what you might say next rather than listening, and judging yourself. Remind yourself that this present moment is all there is. What is happening now is simply happening. When asked, "Are you aware?" or, "Where is your mind right now?" you will observe that your mind has a habit of trying to escape from the present moment. However, mindfulness is becoming intentionally and fully aware of your thoughts and feelings in the present moment.

EXPERIENTIAL EXERCISE—BEING MINDFUL

Stop for a moment. Sit down and become aware of your breathing. Fully accept the present moment. For several minutes, don't try to change anything, just let go and breathe. Breathe and be still. Give yourself permission to let go and allow these moments to be as they are. If that does not work, focus your attention on an object in your surroundings for several minutes. Just pick out an object and stare at it. Now answer the following questions related to the mindfulness exercise you just completed.

What do you love best about your partner?

_____

_____

_____

_____

What do you wish you could tell your partner but have neglected to do so?

_____

_____

_____

_____

What does your partner do that annoys you the most?

_____

_____

_____

_____

One of the reasons your mind attempts to escape the present moment is the fear of being mindful. Your mind would prefer you to be thinking about the past, which you cannot control, and the future, which has not yet, and may never, come. You also need to be aware that mindfulness is a process. Don't get immediately caught up in having a special experience or in making some sort of progress. You will slowly notice differences in your awareness over time.

Affirmations

Affirmations are phrases you can use to reprogram your mind. They are brief statements that put you in the proper frame of mind to accept intuitive inputs. Affirmations are a way of sending your brain a message that the desired result has already been achieved—that what you state, in the present tense, can easily be achieved. Examples of positive affirmations include:

"I am connected to my partner."
"I am sensitive to my partner's needs."
"I am in a relationship with a great partner."
"My partner is my best friend."

EXPERIENTIAL EXERCISE—AFFIRMATIONS
Using the examples above, formulate some of your own affirmations below:

_____
_____
_____
_____
_____
_____
_____

To strengthen your relationship, you need to practice your affirmations on a daily basis. Select one of the affirmations that you feel comfortable with and repeat it for about five minutes each day for one week. For example, if you want to center yourself, you might try repeating the following affirmation: "My partner is my best friend in the world. I can easily talk to my partner about everything." Repeat this affirmation as instructed and then record your observations in the spaces below:

My affirmation is:

_____

_____

_____

_____

My observations include:

_____

_____

_____

_____

My relationship is becoming more effective in the following ways:

_____

_____

_____

_____

_____

_____

_____

Appreciation

Showing appreciation for your partner is critical in building and maintaining an effective relationship. Complete the following statements.

EXPERIENTIAL EXERCISES—APPRECIATION
I appreciate the following characteristics about my partner:

_____
_____
_____
_____
_____
_____
_____
_____

I appreciate the way my partner:

_____
_____
_____
_____
_____
_____
_____
_____

I appreciate the way my partner handled the following situation:

_____

_____

_____

_____

_____

_____

_____

_____

I appreciate my partner for:

_____

_____

_____

_____

_____

_____

_____

_____

Relationship Philosophy

Each partner bring a different philosophy to their relationship. This philosophy develops due to personality traits, parental role models, and childhood history. Answer the following questions to learn more about your, and your partner's, relationship philosophy:

Why do you think that relationships work effectively?

_____

_____

_____

_____

_____

_____

_____

_____

Why do you think that relationships fail?

_____

_____

_____

_____

_____

_____

_____

What was your parent's relationship like? Describe different aspects of their relationship:

_____

_____

_____

_____

What do you remember about the first year of your relationship?

_____

_____

_____

_____

How is your relationship different now from when you were first together?

_____

_____

_____

_____

Why did you and your partner become a couple?

_____

_____

_____

_____

What are your beliefs about children in your relationship?

_____

_____

_____

_____

What are your beliefs about careers in your relationship?

_____

_____

_____

_____

Conflict

Conflict occurs in all relationships. Think about how you and your partner handle conflict, and answer the following questions:

During your last argument . . .

What were you arguing about (finances, hopes, children, fears, etc.)?

_____

_____

_____

_____

What triggered the argument?

_____

_____

_____

_____

What was the outcome of this argument?

_____

_____

_____

_____

What feelings were expressed in this argument?

_____

_____

_____

_____

What was your contribution to the argument?

_____

_____

_____

_____

How could you avoid this type of argument in the future?

_____

_____

_____

_____

What could your partner do to avoid this type of argument in the future?

_____

_____

_____

_____

Sending Emotional Messages

In effective relationships, partners are able to express themselves by sending emotional messages. Complete the following statements to think about the emotional messages you would like to send to your partner:

I get scared when you:

_____

_____

_____

_____

You hurt my feelings when you:

_____

_____

_____

_____

I feel unappreciated when you:

_____

_____

_____

_____

I am sad when you:

_____

_____

_____

_____

I disagree with you about:

_____

_____

_____

_____

I am thankful that you:

_____

_____

_____

_____

I love when you:

_____

_____

_____

_____

I want you to be more:

_____

_____

_____

_____

I get excited when you:

_____

_____

_____

_____

In-Law Issues

All partners in an intimate relationship bring some sort of in-law issues to the union. The following exercise will help you to identify those issues and establish a plan for creating effective coping skills.

Describe your relationship with your partner's family:

_____

_____

_____

_____

On what issues is your partner not on your side?

_____
_____
_____
_____

Describe how you would like your partner to treat your family:

_____
_____
_____
_____

Finances

Finances and financial planning can be major issues in relationships. The ability to confront significant money conflicts is critical to the health of your relationship. Complete the following exercises to determine how much of a problem money presents.

Do you and your partner have a financial plan? Describe it:

_____
_____
_____
_____

How would you describe your approach to money?

_____

_____

_____

_____

How would you describe your partner's approach to money?

_____

_____

_____

_____

How do you wish your partner was in spending and saving money?

_____

_____

_____

_____

What are your long-term financial goals?

_____

_____

_____

_____

What can your partner do to help in meeting this goal?

_____

_____

_____

_____

Plan for Partner Enhancement

Partner enhancement techniques I have utilized in the past:

_____

_____

_____

_____

New enhancement techniques I would like to try with my partner:

_____

_____

_____

_____

Steps I will take to begin using the new enhancement techniques:

_____

_____

_____

_____

When and how I will practice these new enhancement techniques:

_____

_____

_____

_____

Results I hope to achieve:

_____

_____

_____

_____

How I will know when I am successful:

_____

_____

_____

_____

nine

Conflict Resolution

CONSTRUCTIVE CONFLICT RESOLUTION
MEANS GETTING WHAT YOU WANT

Conflict is everywhere—it can't be avoided. It comes up in school, in the workplace, among friends, in the community, and at home. It is an inevitable part of your life, so you must learn how to deal with it effectively. Conflict resolution is a vital part of your personal growth and development, and to be successful in your life and in your career, you must learn more effective conflict resolution skills.

Effective conflict resolution involves working to achieve your goals and get what you need while still maintaining effective relationships with other people. It often results in a negotiating process between you and other people. There is no one best conflict resolution style—different styles can be useful in different situations. Although you don't have to rely on a single, specific style for dealing with conflict, I suggest you get comfortable using one of the styles more often than the others. The Conflict Resolution Style Inventory (CRSI) is designed to help you understand your approach to handling conflict in your life, and to further develop your conflict resolution skills.

CONFLICT RESOLUTION
PREFERENCE INVENTORY

The Conflict Resolution Preference Inventory (CRPI) is designed to help you understand your approach to handling conflict in your life. This inventory contains eighty words divided in to four conflict resolution styles. Read each word, working down the four columns, and decide if the word describes you. If it does, circle that word. If it does not describe you, do not circle the word.

I am:

Analytical	(Leader)	Calm	Spirited
Obliging	Perfectionist	(Dependable)	Strong-willed

In the above examples, the circled words *Leader* and *Dependable* describe the person completing the assessment. Take your time responding, but be sure to respond to every word listed. This is not a test, so there are no right or wrong answers.

I am:

Analytical	Driven	Supportive	Expressive
Detail-oriented	Independent	Amiable	Visionary
Logical	Task-oriented	Dependable	Animated
Low-key	Results-oriented	Relationship-oriented	Energetic
Deep	Decisive	Open	Sociable
Thorough	Dominating	Calm	Spirited
Respectful	Leader	Peaceful	Optimistic
Planner	Dynamic	Reserved	Funny

Perfectionist	Organized	Patient	Inspiring
Orderly	Practical	Shy	Talkative
Withdrawn	Strong-willed	Obliging	Popular
Neat	Confident	Diplomatic	Enthusiastic
Serious	Headstrong	Tolerant	Creative
Introverted	Stubborn	Listener	Playful
Purposeful	Forceful	Permissive	Spontaneous
Economical	Productive	Easygoing	Lively
Solution-oriented	Impatient	Compassionate	Undisciplined
Cautious	Rash	Content	Emotional
Faithful	Outgoing	Friendly	People-oriented
Critical	Take charge	Discreet	Impulsive
I. _____	II. _____	III. _____	IV. _____
TOTAL	TOTAL	TOTAL	TOTAL

SCORING DIRECTIONS

Add the total words circled in each column, then put that total
on the line marked TOTAL at the end of each column. Then,
transfer your totals for each of the four sections to the lines
below:

SECTION I "TOTAL"   =   _____ (Analytical)
SECTION II "TOTAL"   =   _____ (Task-oriented)
SECTION III "TOTAL"   =   _____ (Supportive)
SECTION IV "TOTAL"   =   _____ (Expressive)

INTERPRETING YOUR SCORES

The area in which you scored the highest tends to be the conflict resolution style you most often use. Similarly, the area in which you scored the lowest tends to be your least-used conflict resolution style. To learn more about why you prefer one style more than the others, read the following description of each of the four styles on the CRPI. Please answer the questions related to each of the styles.

SCALE DESCRIPTIONS

SCALE I: ANALYTICAL

People with an Analytical conflict resolution style tend to be very prudent, task-oriented, and focused on the details of the conflict situation in which they find themselves. They are very logical and tend to be very slow, careful decision makers and managers of conflict. They approach conflicts in a low-key manner.

List times when this conflict resolution style has helped you to resolve conflicts in your life:

_____

_____

_____

_____

List times when this conflict resolution style has not worked well for you:

_____

_____

_____

_____

Compare and contrast situations in which your style has and has not worked well. What patterns do you notice?

_____

_____

_____

_____

HOW ANALYTICAL PEOPLE
CAN BE MORE EFFECTIVE

In conflict situations with the other three styles:

With Expressive People
- Use a high level of energy
- Be more spontaneous
- Allow for fun to occur in the process
- See the "big picture"

With Supportive People
- Focus on the other person's feelings
- Don't focus on facts

- Maintain the relationship at all costs
- Forget about using too much logic

With Task-oriented People
- Don't get bogged down in hypothetical situations
- Say what you truly think
- Be results-oriented
- Move at a quick pace

SCALE II: TASK-ORIENTED

People with a Task-oriented conflict resolution style tend to be very independent and decisive. They are task-oriented and like to see instant results when confronted with a conflict situation. They like the conflict resolution process to be fast-paced, and approach conflicts in a domineering manner.

List times when this conflict resolution style has helped you to resolve conflicts in your life:

_____

_____

_____

_____

List times when this conflict resolution style has not worked well for you:

_____

_____

_____

_____

Compare and contrast situations in which your style has and has not worked well. What patterns do you notice?

_____

_____

_____

_____

HOW TASK-ORIENTED PEOPLE CAN BE MORE EFFECTIVE

In conflict situations with the other three styles:

With Expressive People
- Be very warm with the other person
- Focus on feelings
- Be as spontaneous as possible
- Give recognition for their contribution

With Supportive People
- Slow your pace down considerably
- Phrase ideas provisionally
- Be supportive and empathetic
- Show interest in the other person's human side

With Analytical People
- Listen very carefully
- Be cognizant of the importance of details
- Be as logical as you can be
- Don't be too forceful

SCALE III: SUPPORTIVE

People with a Supportive conflict resolution style tend to be very dependable and relationship-oriented. They are very supportive in resolving conflicts with other people. They do not like confrontation and will do anything to avoid it. They tend to be very flexible and approach conflicts in an open manner.

List times when this conflict resolution style has helped you to resolve conflicts in your life:

_____

_____

_____

_____

List times when this conflict resolution style has not worked well for you:

_____

_____

_____

_____

Compare and contrast situations in which your style has and has not worked well. What patterns do you notice?

_____

_____

_____

_____

HOW SUPPORTIVE PEOPLE
CAN BE MORE EFFECTIVE

In conflict situations with the other three styles:

With Expressive People
- Move at a quicker pace
- Be candid and direct
- Focus on the big picture
- Use a high level of energy

With Analytical People
- Be as task-oriented as possible
- Be logical in your conclusions
- De-emphasize feelings
- Be organized and systematic

With Task-oriented People
- Get to the point
- Use a lot of energy
- Focus on the task at hand
- Express your goals and objectives

SCALE IV: EXPRESSIVE

People with an Expressive conflict resolution style tend to be impulsive and have a great deal of energy. They are flamboyant and animated in resolving their conflicts with other people. They can be very talkative and opinionated in their approach to conflict resolution.

List times when this conflict resolution style has helped you to resolve conflicts in your life:

_____

_____

_____

_____

List times when this conflict resolution style has not worked well for you:

_____

_____

_____

_____

Compare and contrast situations in which your style has and has not worked well. What patterns do you notice?

_____

_____

_____

_____

HOW EXPRESSIVE PEOPLE
CAN BE MORE EFFECTIVE

In conflict situations with the other three styles:

With Analytical People
- Listen very carefully
- Don't be too forceful
- Give as much detail as possible
- Give time to make a decision

With Supportive People
- Be open to small talk
- Slow down your pace considerably
- Be supportive and empathetic
- Be aware of the importance of your relationships

With Task-Oriented People
- Be organized in your actions and communications
- Do not get into a power struggle
- Do not engage in small talk
- Do not emphasize feelings

EXERCISES AND ACTIVITIES

An important part of conflict resolution is identifying the situations that create conflict in your life. The following two exercises will help you to learn more about where and when most of your conflicts occur.

WHERE MY CONFLICTS OCCUR

List where and with whom most of your conflicts occur (e.g., in your house, with a significant other, at school, at work, with friends, with your parents, etc.)

WHERE THEY OCCUR	WITH WHOM THEY OCCUR

WHEN MY CONFLICTS OCCUR

List when most of your conflicts occur (e.g., after a sporting event, when you are asked to do something, when you are tired, when you are singled out to do something, etc.) and what you dislike about the situation that causes the conflict.

WHEN THEY OCCUR	WHAT YOU DISLIKE ABOUT THE SITUATION

Identify a major interpersonal conflict that you have been involved in during the past year. This conflict could have been with your parents, brother, sister, peer, significant other, co-worker, boss, or teacher.

Conflict Situation: _____
_____

What strategy or conflict resolution style did you use?

_____
_____
_____
_____

What did you want out of the situation?

_____
_____
_____
_____

How effectively was the conflict resolved?

_____
_____
_____
_____

What strategies did you use to resolve the conflict?

_____

_____

_____

_____

CONFLICT RESOLUTION PATTERNS

List five major conflicts that you can remember throughout your life. What strategies did you use and how effective were the results?

CONFLICTS	HOW THE CONFLICT WAS RESOLVED

What patterns do you see emerging?

_____

_____

_____

_____

The Conflict Resolution Process

Developing your skills in the conflict resolution process can significantly enhance your success and happiness in life. Think back to a conflict you recently had with someone. Use the steps below as an example of an effective process you might have used to resolve the conflict.

Conflict Situation:

_____

_____

_____

Parties Involved:

_____

_____

_____

STEP 1: EACH PERSON DESCRIBES WHAT HE OR SHE WANTS.

What did you want?

_____

_____

What did the other party want?

_____

_____

STEP 2: EACH PERSON DESCRIBES HOW HE OR SHE FEELS ABOUT THE SITUATION.

How did you feel about the situation?

_____

_____

How did the other party feel about the situation?

_____

_____

STEP 3: EACH PERSON EXPLAINS HIS OR HER REASONS FOR WHAT HE OR SHE WANTS IN THE SITUATION.

What were your reasons for what you wanted?

_____

_____

What were the other party's reasons for what they wanted?

_____

_____

STEP 4: EACH PERSON ATTEMPTS TO UNDERSTAND WHAT THE OTHER PERSON WANTS AND HOW HE OR SHE FEELS.

What do you think the other party wanted?

_____

_____

What do you think the other party thought you wanted?

_____

_____

STEP 5: EACH PERSON "BRAINSTORMS" POTENTIAL AGREEMENTS THAT WOULD BE BENEFICIAL TO BOTH PEOPLE.

What were some of the potential solutions that would have benefited both parties?

_____

_____

STEP 6: EACH PERSON CHOOSES THE AGREEMENT THAT SEEMS THE BEST FOR BOTH PEOPLE.

What agreement was chosen? Did it meet both party's needs?

_____

_____

STEP 7: BOTH PEOPLE AGREE TO ABIDE BY THE CONDITIONS OF THE AGREEMENT.

How did both parties agree and did they abide by the agreement?

_____

_____

ten

Emotional Triggers

DON'T LET YOUR EMOTIONS RUN YOU!

Emotions are very complex things. For example, when you experience an emotion such as anger, several different responses occur almost simultaneously. Almost inevitably, thoughts like, "This is not fair," or, "I always get in trouble," rise to the surface. In addition to thoughts, you may experience a variety of physical urges including the desire to hit something, purchase something, or get away from the situation. There may also be a physiological component such as crying or shaking. It's because emotions are so complicated they are extremely difficult to effectively control.

The most recent developments in emotional management have come from the field of cognitive psychology. Cognitive psychologists believe that it is not situations or other people that cause anger. Rather, they suggest that your emotions are actually the consequence of what you *think* about an event. When something happens to you, you begin to think about what happened, you make an evaluation, and only then do emotions occur. In other words, as you interact with your environment, you first think about what is happening to you, experience certain emotions, and then react physically. The conclusion is that it is possible for you to control your emotions by controlling your thinking. You can actually learn to control your emotions by developing new and more effective ways of thinking and behaving. The Emotional Triggers Scale (ETS) is designed to help you to explore what is happening in your life when your thinking triggers negative emotions.

EMOTIONAL TRIGGERS SCALE

This assessment contains thirty statements related to your emotional triggers. Read each of the statements and decide whether or not it describes you. If the statement *does* describe you, circle the number next to that item under the "yes" column. If the statement *does not* describe you, circle the number next to that item under the "no" column.

In the following example, the circled number under the "Yes" column indicates the statement is descriptive of the person completing the inventory.

	YES	NO	
I am considered inflexible.	①	2	(S)

At the end of the inventory, you'll be asked to find the sum total of the numbers you circled in the (S), (O), and (W) categories, respectively. You will get a total in the range from 10 to 20 for each. This is not a test. Since there are no right or wrong answers, do not spend too much time thinking about your answers. Be sure to respond to every statement.

	YES	NO	
I am considered inflexible.	1	2	(S)
I don't like to listen to the opinions of others.	2	1	(S)
I think too critically about myself.	2	1	(S)
I am uncomfortable when I am not in control of things.	1	2	(S)
I worry too much about my public image.	2	1	(S)
I strive to have a perfect reputation.	1	2	(S)
I have a great desire to appear successful.	2	1	(S)
I get upset if I cannot do something as well as I want.	2	1	(S)
I am rarely satisfied.	1	2	(S)
I feel like I must always have the approval of others in my life.	1	2	(S)
I get angry when others are unfair.	1	2	(O)
I get upset if others are late.	2	1	(O)
I get frustrated when others let me down.	2	1	(O)
I worry when someone makes a decision that affects me.	2	1	(O)
I am quick to point out mistakes made by others.	1	2	(O)
I don't receive feedback from others well.	2	1	(O)
When others treat me poorly, they deserve to be punished.	1	2	(O)
It doesn't bother me when others make noises that interrupt me.	2	1	(O)
I get angry when others do not give me the credit I deserve.	1	2	(O)
I am often impatient with incompetent people.	2	1	(O)
Life should always be carefree and easy.	1	2	(W)

I get angry if I am caught in traffic.	2	1	(W)
I get frustrated if events do not go as I plan.	1	2	(W)
There should never be any pain in my life.	1	2	(W)
I get frustrated when technology does not work.	1	2	(W)
I get angry if the weather interferes with activities I have planned.	2	1	(W)
I get irritated when things are not done quickly enough.	1	2	(W)
I can easily cope with changes in my life.	2	1	(W)
I get angry when I have to wait in line.	1	2	(W)
I often compare myself with other people.	2	1	(W)

SCORING DIRECTIONS

Now, add the numbers that you circled that are indicated with an (S) to get your Expectations of Self score. You will get a total in the range from 10 to 20. Put that number in the space marked next to the "Expectations of Self Total" below. Do the same for the other two scales: "(O) Expectations of Others," and "(W) Expectations about the World."

(S) EXPECTATIONS OF SELF TOTAL = _____
(O) EXPECTATIONS OF OTHERS TOTAL = _____
(W) EXPECTATIONS ABOUT THE WORLD TOTAL = _____

To get your overall Emotions Triggers total, add together your (S), (O), and (W) scores. Total scores will range from 30 to 60. Put that score in the space provided below.

NEGATIVE EMOTIONS TRIGGERS TOTAL = _____

INTERPRETING YOUR SCORES

SCORES FROM 17 TO 20 IN ANY SINGLE AREA, OR A TOTAL SCORE FROM 51 TO 60, ARE HIGH and indicate that you do not have many irrational thoughts that cause you to get angry.

SCORES FROM 14 TO 16 IN ANY SINGLE AREA, OR A TOTAL SCORE FROM 40 TO 50, ARE AVERAGE and indicate that you have some irrational thoughts that cause you to get angry, but not too many to be harmful in your life and in your career.

SCORES FROM 10 TO 13 IN ANY SINGLE AREA, OR A TOTAL SCORE FROM 30 TO 39, ARE LOW and indicate that you have many irrational thoughts that cause you to get angry, and can affect your personal and professional success.

SCALE DESCRIPTIONS

(S) EXPECTATIONS OF SELF

Irrational expectations you have about yourself can affect your feelings of anger. Low scores on this scale suggest that you have irrational expectations related to your abilities, intellect, achievement, and success.

(O) EXPECTATIONS OF OTHERS

Irrational expectations you have about others can affect your emotional reactions. Low scores on this scale suggest that you have irrational expectations about intimacy with significant others, support from others, and disappointments with other people in your life.

(W) EXPECTATIONS ABOUT THE WORLD

Irrational expectations you have about the world can affect your negative feelings. Low scores on this scale suggest that you have irrational expectations about traffic, weather, a lack of organization in the world, and why certain things keep happening to you.

EXERCISES AND ACTIVITIES

Regardless of your scores on the ETS, the following exercises have been designed to help you explore your irrational and distorted thinking and make changes so that you can begin to think and react more realistically.

Our Thinking Determines Our Feelings

As we've established, how we react emotionally depends on our thinking. Therefore, when we get angry, it is often because of our expectations for the situation. You must begin to examine your thought patterns to understand what is triggering your angry feelings. These thought patterns are often referred to as self-talk: the words that pop into your head as if you are having a conversation with yourself. By understanding the self-talk that is prompting your anger, you can change your thought patterns that result in angry feelings. You need to learn to let go of certain types of thinking if you are going to control your emotions and your reactions to things and people in your life.

You learned to think in these irrational ways just as you learned to speak a language or play a sport. But the good news is, if you learned to think irrationally, you can learn new thinking patterns, too. To break this habit, you just need to learn new habits!

Emotional Situations

Why do some situations make you emotionally upset, yet others do not? Some people are able to stay calm in certain situations, while others break into an uncontrollable rage. Some situations cause us to feel personally attacked while others do not. There are a great many different types of triggers for negative emotions. What triggers each person's emotional reactions is unique, based on what that person has come to expect of himself, of other people, and of the world in general. It is important for you to explore and revise your unrealistic and irrational expectations in all three of these categories.

EXPECTATIONS OF MYSELF

The irrational expectations you have about yourself can affect your feelings of anger. Complete the following exercise to explore these expectations.

IRRATIONAL EXPECTATIONS OF MYSELF	FEELINGS CAUSED BY THESE EXPECTATIONS

Expectations of Self

PHYSICAL PERFORMANCE

Describe the sports or other physical tasks where you expect more of yourself than you can deliver:

_____

_____

_____

_____

How can you alter your thinking so that you are more realistic?

_____

_____

_____

_____

INTELLECTUAL PURSUITS

Describe the intellectual tasks where you expect more of yourself than you can deliver:

_____

_____

_____

_____

How can you alter your thinking so that you are more realistic?

_____

_____

_____

_____

DEADLINES

Describe the situations in which you have deadlines where you expect more of yourself than you can deliver:

_____

_____

_____

_____

How can you alter your thinking so that you are more realistic?

_____

_____

_____

_____

SUCCESSES/ACHIEVEMENTS

Describe the areas of success and achievements where you expect more of yourself than you can deliver:

_____

_____

_____

_____

How can you alter your thinking so that you are more realistic?

_____

_____

_____

_____

SPIRITUALITY

Describe the spiritual tasks where you expect more of yourself than you can deliver:

_____

_____

_____

_____

How can you alter your thinking so that you are more realistic?

_____

_____

_____

_____

EXPECTATIONS OF OTHERS

The irrational expectations you have about others can affect your emotional reactions. Complete the following exercise to explore these expectations.

IRRATIONAL EXPECTATIONS OF OTHERS	FEELINGS CAUSED BY THESE EXPECTATIONS

MANNERS

Describe the unwritten rules of etiquette people break that upset you:

_____

_____

_____

_____

How can you alter your thinking so that you are more realistic?

_____

_____

_____

_____

DISAPPOINTMENTS

Describe the disappointing things people do that evoke your negative emotions:

_____

_____

_____

_____

How can you alter your thinking so that you are more realistic?

_____

_____

_____

_____

SUPPORT

Describe how a lack of support from others causes you to get upset:

_____

_____

_____

_____

How can you alter your thinking so that you are more realistic?

_____

_____

_____

_____

INTIMACY

Describe how a lack of intimacy evokes negative emotions in you:

_____

_____

_____

_____

How can you alter your thinking so that you are more realistic?

_____

_____

_____

_____

INTRUSIONS

Describe how intrusions on your time cause you to become upset:

_____

_____

_____

_____

How can you alter your thinking so that you are more realistic?

_____

_____

_____

_____

EXPECTATIONS OF THE WORLD

The irrational expectations you have about the world can affect your negative feelings. Complete the following exercise to explore these expectations.

IRRATIONAL EXPECTATIONS OF THE WORLD	FEELINGS CAUSED BY THESE EXPECTATIONS

ELECTRONIC DEVICES

Describe how computers and other electronic devices make you mad:

_____

_____

_____

_____

How can you alter your thinking so that you are more realistic?

_____

_____

_____

_____

LACK OF ORGANIZATION

Describe how things not organized to your liking irritate you:

_____

_____

_____

_____

How can you alter your thinking so that you are more realistic?

_____

_____

_____

_____

CHANGE

Describe the situations in which sudden changes cause you to be angry:

_____

_____

_____

_____

How can you alter your thinking so that you are more realistic?

_____

_____

_____

_____

TRAFFIC

Describe how traffic conditions evoke negative emotions in you:

_____

_____

_____

_____

How can you alter your thinking so that you are more realistic?

_____

_____

_____

_____

WEATHER

Describe how changes in the weather upset you:

_____

_____

_____

_____

How can you alter your thinking so that you are more realistic?

_____

_____

_____

_____

Progressive Muscle Relaxation

Progressive muscle relaxation helps you to bring relaxation to all parts of your body through concentrated awareness. This relaxation technique helps to reduce anger and provides you with a system for stopping the escalation of emotions in your daily life. Progressive relaxation allows you to actually ease tension by focusing self-suggestions of warmth and relaxation in specific muscle groups throughout the body.

EXPERIENTIAL EXERCISE: PROGRESSIVE MUSCLE RELAXATION
Sit in a comfortable position. Close your eyes and start to feel your body relaxing. Think of yourself as a rag doll, and let the relaxation pass through each organ and body part. In this exercise, start with your feet and progressively relax all the parts of your body. This technique will help you to manage your emotions effectively.

You can start with such statements as:

"I am relaxing my feet. . . . My feet are warm. . . . My feet are relaxed."

"I am relaxing my ankles. . . . My ankles are warm. . . . My ankles are relaxed."

"I am relaxing my calves. . . . My calves are warm. . . . My calves are relaxed."

"I am relaxing my knees. . . . My knees are warm. . . . My knees are relaxed."

"I am relaxing my thighs. . . . My thighs are warm. . . . My thighs are relaxed."

Repeat with the rest of your body until you are totally relaxed from your head to your feet. Block any distractions out of your mind as you concentrate on relaxing your entire body.

Meditation

Meditation is the practice of focusing your attention on one thing at a time. It is a method that uses repeated mental focus to quiet your mind, which in turn quiets your body—focusing on one thing allows your mind to stay concentrated and excludes all other thoughts.

There are many different forms of meditation. You can meditate by repeating a word like "Om," counting your breaths after you exhale, or gazing at an object like a candle or a piece of wood without thinking about it in words.

Thought Control

Whenever you start to feel unwanted emotions, you can examine your thinking by first stopping what you are saying and doing. Do not push your thoughts away or ignore them, simply stop in your tracks. Then, explore what you are saying to yourself. Remember that what you say to yourself can either calm you down or make you more emotional.

Try not to say things like:

"Who is he or she to treat me like this?"
"Life's not fair."
"Just my luck."

"This is not fair!"
"This should not be happening to me."
"I don't deserve this."

Try to say things like:

"I don't have to take this personally."
"They are entitled to their opinion."
"I will react differently this time."
"This is a challenge, not a problem."
"Life isn't always fair."
"These types of things happen to all people."

Listen To Music

Listening to music is one of the best and most accessible forms of relaxation. Select music that is soothing and peaceful. To benefit the most from your music relaxation sessions, you should dedicate approximately 30 minutes of uninterrupted time to yourself daily.

IDENTIFY THE PHYSICAL SIGNS

You should start to track the physical signs and symptoms that occur just before you begin to feel certain unwanted emotions. These warning signals may include such things as rapid breathing and increased pulse rate.

EMOTION-PRODUCING SITUATIONS	PHYSICAL SIGNS AND SYMPTOMS

KEEP AN EMOTIONAL DIARY

It would be helpful to start keeping a record of when you experience unwanted emotions, what situation brings the feelings on, and who you are with. This exercise will help you identify emotional patterns in your life.

WHEN DID I GET EMOTIONAL?	WHAT WAS THE SITUATION?	WHO WAS I WITH?

CONCLUDING FAQs

Whenever I finish conducting a Life Skills IQ workshop, people inevitably come up to me and ask questions. Sometimes it's a case of not wanting to ask in front of other people, but other times, it's simply a matter of people thinking of questions only after they've completed the assessments and journal exercises. I suspect that now that you have completed the assessments in this book and learned more about yourself, you might have questions about what you have just worked on. Because you are unable to ask me personally, I'm going to provide answers to some of the most frequently asked life skills questions.

How Would You Describe Life Skills?

Life skills are the skills you need to be successful in your career and your relationships. Essential life skills include such things as communicating effectively with other people, being assertive enough to stand up for your rights, managing your time well, resolving conflicts so that both parties win, and managing your money well. Life skills are a necessary component of effectively managing change in your environment, dealing effectively with your environment and the people in it, and taking charge of your professional and personal life. They're particularly critical because unlike traditional intelligence, life skills can be learned and developed over time.

What Types of Intelligences Make up My Life Skills IQ?
Your Life Skills IQ is comprised of many components including Spiritual, Physical, Mental, Emotional, Social, and Career intelligences. Hopefully, you have been able to assess and explore all of these types of intelligences by taking the life skills assessments in this book.

What Are Life Skills Patterns?
Have you ever been frustrated because you keep reliving negative events in your life? If so, you are not alone. Life skills patterns are the behaviors, whether positive or negative, that you keep repeating over and over again regardless of the results you get.

How Is My Life Skills IQ Determined?
Your Life Skills IQ is determined by the degree of your effectiveness in identifying and applying proactive life skills. When you are successful, you naturally tend to keep doing what works well. Successful people manage their time and money well, communicate effectively with others, resolve conflicts and make good decisions, and manage their emotions well. These people, whose patterns allow them to be effective and efficient in life, have a high Life Skills IQ. One the other hand, people who keep repeating patterns that are not effective and efficient see their lives start to break down. These negative life skills patterns are indicated by having trouble maintaining relationships with other people, experiencing career problems, feeling like you cannot get a lot done, giving up easily, trying to avoid other things in your life, and lacking an overall sense of flow in life. If this is happening, you have a low Life Skills IQ.

My hope is that, by completing the assessments contained in this book, you have learned a great deal about both yourself and your Life Skills IQ. You have learned more about your life skills strengths and your life skills weaknesses. Now, it's time for you to really put them to work.

How Can I Break Negative Patterns and Raise My Life Skills IQ?

Whether or not they are effective in helping you achieve your goals, your life skills patterns will continue repeating themselves if they are left unexamined. That's the reason so many people go through life using ineffective life skills over and over again and expecting different results each time. The key lies in self-reflection, the kind you engage in when you take the assessments in this book. Once you have identified your negative patterns, you will have the power to alter them so that you begin to experience positive results rather than negative ones. The goal of this book is to help you reflect on the negative patterns in your life and find alternative behaviors to help you identify more effective choices.

How Does Self-Reflection Work?

The art of self-reflection goes back many centuries and is rooted in many of the world's greatest spiritual and philosophical traditions. Socrates, the ancient Greek philosopher, was known to walk the streets engaging the people he met in philosophical reflection and dialogue. He felt this type of activity was so important in life that he went so far as to proclaim that "The unexamined life is not worth living!" We can think of "the unexamined life" as a life with negative life skills patterns that people repeat over and over again without ever thinking about how life should really be lived.

When you are unreflective, simply reacting to life's occurrences, you miss out on life's deeper meanings and patterns. You forgo your capacity to think about important issues and develop realistic conclusions about yourself and your place in the world. You allow yourself to live on automatic pilot, following the views you acquired early in life. When you lead an unexamined life, you choose not to make use of your uniquely human capacity to reflect and think deeply about yourself and the patterns you currently live by.

Why Do Human Beings Lead Unexamined Lives?
The answer is that we seem to fear self-reflection and self-examination. However, a structured reflection and examination of your beliefs, assumptions, characteristics, and patterns will help you know yourself better, which will lead to a more satisfying life and career. A greater level of self-understanding about life skills is necessary to make positive, self-directed changes to the negative patterns you keep repeating in life.

Where Do I Go from Here?
Now that you have become more aware of both the positive and negative life skills patterns in your life, you have successfully moved them from your unconscious mind to your conscious thinking. Now you will be able to calmly and patiently monitor your thoughts and actions. When you encounter a situation that requires a particular life skill, you will be able to see things for how they really are, and act appropriately.

Finally, please remember the assessments in this book are not designed to take the place of psychological services. If you feel you are unable to cope with specific life situations, please consult a mental health professional immediately.